THE FORTEAN TIMES BOOK OF

Exploding Pigs

and other strange
animal stories

THE FORTEAN TIMES BOOK OF

Exploding Pigs

and other strange
animal stories

COMPILED BY IAN SIMMONS

ILLUSTRATED BY ED TRAQUINO

JOHN BROWN PUBLISHING

First published in Great Britain in October 1997
by John Brown Publishing Ltd, 136/142 Bramley Road,
Ladbroke Grove, London W10 6SR, UK.
Tel 0171 565 3000.

ISBN 1-870870-360

Layout and editing by James Wallis
Printed and bound in Great Britain by
Creative Print and Design (Wales), Ebbw Vale

CONTENTS

Animals are a source of endless fascination to people, which is, I suppose, one of the main reasons we keep pets. Pet owners love nothing better than to hold forth on the quirks and eccentricities of their charges, and then there's wildlife programmes, where the latest Attenborough-fronted revelations about the private life of something in the Namib Desert can top the ratings for weeks on end. It is, I imagine, the infinite variety of things animals will do which keeps our attention. They can be amazingly human in their behaviour one moment, utterly alien the next; cute and funny one minute, then suddenly bizarre and sinister. They seem to know what we are thinking, appear to have hidden abilities we cannot understand, and often lead us to suspect that they might be conspiring against us behind our backs — the "Far Side" cartoon of cows standing on their hind legs reading newspapers, who, at the shout of "CAR!", drop to all fours and start munching grass captures this uneasy feeling perfectly.

It is not surprising, then, that our newspapers and magazines are packed with items about animals, champion dogs, rescued strays, Humphrey the Downing Street cat — they all get column inches. Needless to say, as a result the *Fortean Times* clipping files contain huge quantities of animal-related reports from across the globe, guaranteed to be weirder and more baffling than anything you ever dreamed could be possible — woodpeckers disabling spacecraft, iguanas driving cars, cats destroying houses and lumberjacks raping dead raccoons, they are all there. Many of the classic tales that follow have appeared in the *Fortean Times* over the years. Many have not, however, due to limitations of space, so it has been a great pleasure to go back through the archives and resurrect them here to give an overview of the whole spectrum of Fortean animal behaviour.

Whether every tale is one hundred per cent true, though, I cannot say for sure — newspapers often use animal tales as filler items and are not above exaggerating for comic effect or re-running old stories with the names and locations changed. Some quite happily report obvious urban legends as fact. We do not have the resources to follow up all our stories and verify the reports we receive, but all the incidents in here have been reported as true in the news media and at the back you will find a list of the sources for each of the stories should you need to check back for yourself. Where something seems likely to be an urban legend I have mentioned this in the text.

This book would not exist without the dedication and sharp scissors of the legion of clipsters who go through papers the world over and send us news of the surreal goings-on in their part of the world. It is thanks to them that we can call upon weirdness from the *Uganda Star*, *O Globo*, *The South China Morning Post* and many others to bring you the best in world-wide forteana. I owe a great debt to all of them. Thanks are also due to our cat, Little My, for constant first-hand reminders of the strangeness and perversity of animals.

Ian Simmons

Beasts Bite Back

Humanity is notorious for its assaults on the animal kingdom. Just sometimes, though, the boot is on the other foot.

SHEEP are notoriously passive and helpless, or so they would have us believe. Sometimes, though, the evidence suggests otherwise. Research in New Zealand has shown that one-third of farmers had been seriously injured in attacks by sheep, often being charged from behind and receiving damaged knees and broken vertebrae from the aggressive beasts.

Closer to home, near Nottingham, parachutist Alison Pearson, 28, made a 13,500-feet drop without incident — until she landed in a field full of sheep and received serious chest injuries from being charged by a Suffolk-cross ewe panicked by her sudden arrival. In Merthyr Tydfil, Wales, meanwhile, gangs of sheep from the local hills have taken to hanging out in the car-park of the ASDA supermarket. They menace customers in order to get fed, and flocks of them follow people to their cars and nose about in the boot as groceries are loaded. They are particularly fond of fresh cakes and French bread, although ice-cream is also popular.

COWS too are thought to be peaceable beasts – but what can we make of the following incident, which took place in Cortina d'Ampezzo, Italy? The municipal brass band were marching through the outskirts of the town when a herd of 25 cows burst out of their field and butted the musicians to the ground, then stood around licking their instruments affectionately. It took an hour to drive the animals away.

IN NORWAY a skier being savaged by an elk saved himself by ramming two fingers up its nose, making it faint.

WILLIAM FAUST, 25, of Torrence, California, pulled off the road in Topanga Canyon for a quick pee on a rural building site. While there he kicked idly at some plywood and fell into a 30ft-deep cesspit. Not long after, a gopher fell in as well and started attacking Faust. "It kept charging me," he said. "I had to fend it off all night." Workmen rescued both in the morning.

ANOTHER RODENT created an arcane footnote to the Pied Piper legend in 1982. Teenager Glen Aspinal, from Barnsley, was on a British army adventure holiday in Hamelin, Germany, when he was bitten by a three-legged mouse and had to undergo a course of injections as a precaution against rabies. "We had wanted to keep the mouse to carry out tests for rabies," said an army spokesman, "but it escaped from the guardroom where we had locked it in."

VICAR Stephen Grey, of St Michael's Church, Bamford, showed bravery comparable to that of any martyr when he continued his prayers after a ferret rocketed up his cassock. Rev. Grey was alerted to the intruder when a woman worshipper screamed and jumped up on a pew. "I looked up, and there it was, staring at me," Rev. Grey said. "It went three times around my cassock and then stuck its head underneath." Eventually the ferret was ejected from the church after biting a parishioner's thumb. "I was trained to carry on regardless, but I must admit the prayers speeded up a bit towards the end," said Rev. Grey.

SEAFOOD is known for violently disagreeing with people, but not often in quite this way. Maine resident Mark Labbe was returning home from the seafood store with a live lobster he had just bought when it escaped from its sack and started to bite his leg. As he bent over to pick it up, his Buick swerved into oncoming traffic and collided with Lisa Brown's Plymouth, causing $300 of damage to each car.

An even more savage assault was suffered by Benito Feroldi as he made a scuba dive off the Italian Riviera. Tempted by a school of lobsters, he swam over and tried to grab one, but it turned on him and lashed out, slashing his arms and chest and bashing him against rocks before he dragged it back to his boat. Locals were amazed, and said lobsters had never gone on the rampage like this before.

Thankfully, assaults by enraged crustacea are not common in Britain, but a 1995 survey of Scottish hospital casualty records revealed the first known incidence of a hospital visit occasioned by a prawn biting a human.

ANOTHER UNDERWATER ASSAULT killed swimmer Stephen Sheehan off Queensland, Australia. He was struck on the head by a cod, which knocked him unconscious. He drowned.

SHARK ATTACKS are a more conventional form of aquatic violence, but even these can have a surprising twist. Wiley Beevers was diving in New Orleans when a six-foot long, 120-pound shark attacked him, tearing into his left arm and causing a wound that needed 75 stitches to close. Not so surprising, perhaps, but this attack took place in Sharkey's Reef fish restaurant in the middle of peak dining hours. Beevers was swimming in the tank, feeding lettuce to the tropical fish, when the tiger shark made its move. Another diver was forced to leap in and haul Beevers out because the blood was driving the other sharks in the tank into a feeding frenzy and they were closing on the injured man to join in. Commenting on the accident, restaurant owner Jack Dunn said, "[The diners] got to see something a lot of people hope they'll never get to see."

NASINE CLOER, 46, had a narrow escape aboard a houseboat off Islamorada in the Florida Keys during a family fishing trip. An eight-foot barracuda hurled itself almost 15 feet out of the water onto the boat, slicing into Nasine's arm, hip and thigh with its razor-sharp teeth. Relatives managed to shove the fish overboard with boathooks, but Mrs Cloer needed 200 stitches, tendon replacements and skin grafts. The barracuda came within an inch of severing an artery, which would have proved fatal. The previous day Bobby Martin of Jemison, Alabama had needed 20 stitches after a 40-pound barracuda pulled the same stunt, leaping into a tourist boat off Bradenton, also in Florida, and sinking its teeth into him. Gainesville biologist George Burgess said, "I never heard of them jumping out the water."

SEAFOOD ATTACKS from the water might be expected, but not from above. However, that is exactly what Steve Hall suffered in Fort Lauderdale, Florida. He nearly wrote off his open-top sports car when a seagull dropped a turtle into his lap. In Sydney, Karen Gilles was also the target of a bird bombing. She was sitting in a playground with a friend, who said, "Look at that bird... it's got something round and white in its mouth." Mrs Gilles looked up, and as she did so the bird let go – causing her to be smashed in the face by a plummeting golf ball, making a gash that needed several stitches. Mrs Gilles' amused workmates had the ball mounted on a plaque.

ELSEWHERE birds took a more direct route in their assaults. In Tenerife a rare griffon vulture reduced a football match to disarray by repeatedly swooping onto the pitch and attacking the referee and players, while in the woods of America's Pacific north-west joggers with ponytails are at risk. According to *Playboy* magazine, barred owls "were mistaking the ponytailed heads of runners for squirrels." One victim said, "It's when they are just waking up. They're hungry and grumpy, and to them your head looks like a giant hamburger."

EARLY ONE MORNING Duncan Whyte was helping colleagues at Bowmore Distillers in Linlithgow, Scotland, change a lightbulb in the warehouse where they were working. Because they needed to turn the power off, Duncan went to fetch a torch. No sooner had he stepped out the door when his colleagues heard a terrible yell and saw Duncan stagger back in, clutching his head in distress. When he was asked what had happened he woozily led them outside to show them what had almost flattened him – there, lying on the ground, was a full-grown swan. The bird had been blown off course by high winds and had hit overhead wires. It had then bounced off the warehouse roof and crashed onto Duncan's head. Duncan proved to be unhurt apart from a stiff neck and was fine after a lie-down, but the swan had been killed by the impact.

A PELICAN exhibited an exquisite sense of timing in Los Angeles. It shat on Benny Subo's head as he proposed to his girlfriend. Benny sued the marina where it happened.

A FALCON swooped down on an elderly visitor to the Milky Way Falconry in North Devon and grabbed his toupee, carrying the furry object off to his perch – presumably to eat it, or at least to try. The falconer swiftly retrieved the hairpiece, but it was unwearable.

DENTURES proved to be the favoured prosthesis of a crow in Norway. Agnes Lysholm, 81, lost her dentures after she tried to spit out a fishbone which had become jammed in her throat. A crow swooped down, grabbed them and disappeared. Mrs Lysholm gave the teeth up for lost, but six days later her son Kristian saw a magpie in a nearby tree holding something in its beak, which he realised was the missing denture. As he ran outside, the magpie dropped it and flew off. Said Agnes, "This is almost supernatural... it seems that it was arranged by 'small invisible men'."

IN OMAN a cock made an even more direct attack. Instead of seizing for a prosthesis it went direct for a more firmly attached item – an ear. A man named only as Jamal was walking through the town of Kalamassery when a huge cock weighing more than 10kg flew at him, landed on his shoulder, wrenched his ear off, then flew to safety before anyone could catch it.

DOMESTIC PETS are no slouch at creating havoc either. Trixie, a four-year-old mongrel, blew her owner's house right off its foundations by pulling at a taper used to light the cooker. This left an open-ended pipe pouring gas into the room, which was ignited by the pilot light and caused a massive explosion. Trixie and her owners miraculously escaped unhurt, but the house had to be completely rebuilt. In Plymouth a cat pulled a similar trick: two fire engines were needed to put out a fire that started when a kitten turned up the heat under a chip pan with its paw.

POSTMEN in Beccles, Suffolk, live in fear of the savage creature that lurks at Mike Smith-Howell's house, and he has been warned that the Royal Mail may not continue to deliver his mail unless his aggressive pet is brought under control. This is no slavering Rottweiler, however: it is Gizmo, a small black cat which sits at the bottom of the stairs every morning, waiting for the post. As soon as she hears the postman's footsteps, she leaps to the door and claws at any fingers that come through the letterbox. So far she has mauled six postmen, two parcel-delivery men and several teenagers delivering junk mail. The last straw came when she shredded an unsuspecting relief postman who did not notice the 'Caution, killer cat' sign, and Mr Smith-Howell has now been asked to put a box outside for his mail.

A HIPPO caused havoc along the Niger river in West Africa, attacking canoes and destroying rice fields. Villagers in Mali hunted the beast in vain for months. Many believed it had magical powers of flight and invisibility.

FAHED SUBITAN, an Arab worker on Israel's only crocodile farm, in the Jordan Valley, tripped over a hosepipe as he fled from an angry 12ft female. As he lay sprawled on the ground, expecting the worst, there was a ringing – his mobile phone had fallen from his pocket when he fell, and his girlfriend had chosen that moment to call him. The croc paused, looked at Subitan, looked at the phone, swallowed the latter, and then turned round and retreated to her pool, satisfied. Gloria Gaber, the farm manager said, "Afterwards we rang the number, but all we got was the busy signal."

A HERD of zebras surrounded a minibus carrying students in south-eastern Kenya, and started kicking it. They stopped only when another minibus driver threw a bottle of water over them. A game warden said he'd never heard of zebras behaving so aggressively.

BILL TURNER, 81, was watering his fruit trees near Perth in Australia when he was attacked by a 5ft 6in kangaroo. It punched and clawed Bill as he wrestled it to the ground. He tried to cross its arms and break them – a recommended technique, apparently – but the roo just bit him savagely in return. Desperate to escape, Bill grabbed the bounder by the balls and gave them a good twist. This did the trick, the roo let go and Bill was able to flee to the house. He had to have 50 stitches in the cuts and bites all over his body. Police shot the roo.

Touch of Mystery

Animal behaviour is sometimes startlingly
human-like, but at other times it is so
incomprehensible as to be utterly baffling.

A HUNDRED AND TWENTY baboons had a three-day
stand-off with their keepers in Emmen Zoo, Holland in
1994, when they refused to come down from the trees in
their compound. The normally ground-dwelling Hamadryas
baboons took to the trees en masse one Sunday and stayed
there, refusing to return to ground level under any circumstances except one — when keepers put out food for the apes
they would descend, but would quickly grab the items
before rushing back to their perches to eat it. Then, after

three days, the apes all descended to the ground again and continued as if nothing had happened. Everyone was completely baffled as to what had caused the apes to behave so strangely. One of the more unlikely suggestions was that they were influenced by the comet Shoemaker-Levy colliding with Jupiter, which occurred at the same time.

NORWICH'S CHIEF public health officer, Tony Welch, recorded an extraordinary discovery in his 1982 annual report – deep-freeze mice. He reported the discovery of six mice dwelling in a deep freeze in the city. They had long woolly coats and survived by gnawing on food in the freezer, even though it was frozen solid – they even thrived on the rat poison left out for them. Welch said, "They didn't mind how cold it got. I've never seen anything like it." His staff, however, ensured they did not prosper for long.

ALSO IN NORWICH, a flock of swans on the River Wensum caused consternation when they all turned bright blue. Baffled RSPCA inspectors were trying to catch them to solve the mystery.

MOTHS in the Ewden Valley near Stocksbridge, Yorkshire created a ghost-tree by swathing it in silk. A large number of small ermine moths cocooned the entire tree in a layer of silk from the base of its trunk to the tips of its branches in order to breed. Conservationist Andy Warren examined the tree. "It's incredible," he said. "I have never seen anything like it." He explained that it must have taken tens of thousands of the tiny white moths to cover an entire tree: "Usually they take over a small bush, not a tree, they weave the silk as a protective cover from other insects and to act as camouflage."

THE THEOSOPHICAL REVIEW recorded a number of extraordinary animal tales from the press in the early part of the century. One comes from the *Daily Telegraph* of 14 October 1902 came this one. It relates to a snail farmer in the canton of Vaud in the Jura. He kept his edible snails, up to 50,000 at a time, in an enclosure surrounded by a wooden fence three feet high, which was topped by a board edged with metal spikes to prevent the molluscs escaping. The snails, however, worked out how to get round this. A number of them would climb the side of the enclosure until they reached the top, then they formed their bodies into a sort of ladder so that those behind could pass over the shells of the others. This enabled them to get out of the enclosure with only one of their number getting impaled on a spike.

BULGARIAN FARMER Mihail Janko believed his goat could tell 'goodies' from 'baddies'. It butted pictures of unpleasant characters and tried to eat photographs of nice people. Mihail put this talent to good use by using his goat to select suitors for his four daughters and to vet tradesman trying to sell him things.

ANOTHER GOAT was rather less welcome when it appeared in Tipton. Sixteen-year-old Simon Mannering discovered the baby goat one Sunday, sitting in the basket belonging to the family cats, Paddy and Willy, with no obvious sign as to how he had got there. His mother, Dianne, and a woman officer at Tipton police station thought he was joking when he told them – the police woman even asked if he had been drinking, but the goat was there for all to see. The cats were terrified of the animal, which was named Lucifer by the family, and the Mannerings were none too enthusiastic about him either. "We really do not want to keep Lucifer, I'm afraid," said Mrs Mannering. "So we would like to hear from anyone who might have lost a kid recently."

THE BELIEF that the howl of a dog signifies death was apparently borne out by an occurrence in Twickenham in 1876. A lost dog took refuge in the house of a barge-man named Brooks, where it hid under a chair and began to howl frantically. Brooks was absent but his wife let various neighbours gather in the house to see the spectacle. One of them mentioned the old superstition, but the rest laughed it off. They attributed the dog's behaviour to madness, so one of them went for a gun and shot the unfortunate creature. As the animal lay dying a messenger arrived to tell Mrs Brooks that her husband was dying, having had a fit and fallen overboard from his barge.

MORE RECENTLY the experience of Mrs Flo Harris of Deal supported the idea of the ancients that bees were divine messengers and that the soul takes on the form of a bee shortly before death. She explained: "A bee came indoors and just would not go. It flew around as if trying to tell me something, then lay on the window sill as if it were dying. Then my brother came in and said my sister had died."

THE LAKOTA SIOUX believe that when one of them dies a white owl takes their soul to the deity. An un-named clergyman told this story regarding an event in 1984. He was at the bedside of a dying Sioux in a hospital in Omaha, Nebraska, along with the man's wife. After the last rites were completed the old man turned to face the window. The clergyman followed his gaze and saw a little white owl fly against the window and disappear. The wife turned and said, "Owl!" The clergyman looked back at the patient and saw he was dead. White owls are very rare in the area: the clergyman hadn't seen one since he was a child in Kansas.

THE FIJIAN PRESIDENT was said to be a direct descendant of the shark god Dakuwaqa, so it was fitting that a school of sharks should have appeared suddenly in Suva Harbour to accompany the funeral flotilla of Ratu Sir Penaia Ganilau out to sea. The sharks surfaced during the ceremonial 21-gun salute in front of the Tovuto which carried the president's coffin to his home island of Taveuni. In the eyes of the mourner, the sharks' appearance reaffirmed the bloodline from Dakuwaqa. Sightings of even a single shark in Suva Harbour are rare.

DIANA TELLING, 57, was backing out of her drive in Coed-y-Cando, New Inn, South Wales, when a dead pigeon fell on her lawn. Minutes later, while driving past the nearby Rechem factory, another pigeon fell on the road in front of her and she ran over it. A little later she rang her partner in Newport who told her that a dead pigeon had fallen from the sky in front of him as he walked into the town. RSPB spokesman Tony Prater said they had probably succumbed to trichomoniosis, a fatal lung disease in urban pigeons which makes them collapse in mid-air and crash to the ground, but he admitted it was rare to see the birds falling and quite amazing to have two people see it happen on the same day.

HUNDREDS OF STARLINGS were found dead or dying in a remote lane in Anglesey. About 300 birds were found along a 20-yard stretch of road near Bodedern, some heaped on top of each other, others in the hedgerows. Alistair

Moralee, the senior RSPB warden on the island, was baffled and collected specimens for further examination. Theories ranged from poison to the birds being zapped by lightning as they perched on overhead cables. Strangely, a preliminary post-mortem seemed to suggest the bird's livers had been cooked – but not any other internal organs. Another detail puzzled Mr Moralee. "There were no dead birds in the fields on either side of the track," he said. And why only starlings? Maybe W.Hone's *Table Book, Vol 1* from 1827 can throw some light on the event. This records a vast battle between starlings over Yorkshire in 1825, after which 1087 were found dead.

AN EVEN STRANGER bird fall took place near Campeche on the coast of Mexico. Hundreds of birds from as many as sixteen different species were seen crashing to the ground all over the area. They all appeared to be suffering from head injuries which were not the result of colliding with the ground – it seemed as if they had crashed into something solid but invisible in the sky.

HEADLESS SEAGULLS by the hundred were washed up on a beach near Poole, Dorset in July 1995. Authorities were baffled, but a spokesman for the Dorset Wildlife Trust said, "I find it difficult to imagine natural circumstances decapitating birds. It could be mink, but sadly it is always possible it was done by humans."

AUBERON WAUGH mentions coming across a letter in a local newspaper from two men in Sherbourne, Dorset, who were walking along a public footpath near Sherbourne Castle when they saw six hares run headlong in single file into a field with sheep in it. In a large open area all six suddenly stopped simultaneously, then ran in a circle clockwise, stopped, ran anti-clockwise for rather longer, then dashed off, once more in single file, into a wood.

WHILE RENOVATING an old warehouse Chris Peers went into a disused courtyard which had clearly not been entered by humans for a long time. In the middle of the courtyard was a semi-circle of six or eight feral cats, all thin and in poor condition, sitting on their haunches and all apparently looking at another cat in the middle of the semi-circle, sitting and facing them. This animal was very different from the rest. It was well-fed and healthy-looking, and very much larger than the average domestic cat. All the animals had been sitting absolutely motionless until he arrived, but as soon as he did the smaller cats fled in all directions. The large one, however, remained sitting where it was and turned to stare straight at Peers. Because of its size and lack of fear, he believed himself to be in some danger, so he scrambled over a wall and escaped into the street.

MRS B. N. HARRIS of Harrogate in Yorkshire related a strange cat experience she witnessed during World War Two. "During the wartime evacuation from London we were housed in Tiverton Road, Exeter – the straight road out into the country. In the early evening before the tragic raid which so devastated the city, there was an unbelievable exodus of cats, padding in a gentle stream past our window towards Tiverton. Knowing nothing about cats, we watched in great surprise, wondering why. Before morning – sadly we knew."

ACCORDING to T. A. Shellswell, a fox being chased by his local hunt once sought sanctuary in a neglected corner of his garden, later escaping safely. Every year since, wild foxgloves have grown there, where nothing grew before.

CHAPTER THREE

Dumb Animals

There's dumb... and then there's *really* dumb

DEMPSEY THE DOBERMAN had to be rushed to the vet to have his jaws separated after enthusiastically scoffing a tube of superglue in Bournemouth, Dorset.

REUBEN AND EVELYN Storlien of Marietta, Minnesota awoke one morning to find two deer lying in their front yard, antlers locked. One was injured but still alive, the other was a life-size concrete garden ornament which normally stood on the Storliens' lawn. Neither the Storliens or any of their neighbours had been disturbed by the clash during the night, but it seemed the live deer had mistaken the concrete one for a rutting season rival, squared off against it and charged, locking antlers and pulling the statue over on top of himself. The statue's antlers were broken off and entangled in the eight-point rack of the live deer, but the rest of the statue had pinned him immovably to the ground. It took eight men to lift the concrete deer off the live one, but it was too severely injured and had to be destroyed.

AS MACHINE OPERATOR Michael O'Keefe, 44, was being driven to work by his uncle, their car slammed into a 700lb (318kg) moose on a foggy road in north-east Vermont. The accident shattered the windscreen and flattened the roof of the car, but neither man was seriously hurt. The moose was not so lucky and was killed. O'Keefe was treated for cuts and went out again to go apple picking. Five hours later he was driving home, still shaken, when an even bigger moose, an 800lb (364kg) one this time, galloped out of the woods and smashed into the front of his truck on the passenger side. "The antlers caught the top of the truck and the nose hit the windshield," he said. "As he was coming down I yanked my truck from under him so he'd land on the highway." Game warden Paul Fink, who had just delivered the first moose to a slaughterhouse, was called out to kill the badly injured second animal.

A PORCUPINE was the sworn enemy of Mrs Rhodes of Henley-on-Thames, when she lived in the Green Mountains of Vermont, USA. She had a log cabin that the family used for summer breaks: to protect it in the winter, the doors had wire netting nailed over them. This did not deter the porcupine. One winter he ate right through the wire, then chewed his way on through the door and into the cabin. Once in, he ate the head and foot ends of a pair of twin beds and part of a chair. He then added insult to injury by appearing to attack Mrs Rhodes from a tree when she caught up with him and cursed him out the following spring. After that, it's not surprising she moved to Henley-on-Thames.

PETS ARE SUPPOSED to have a calming influence on their owners, but this was not the case for Jean Glover, 40, of Auckland, New Zealand, who took pills to control her heart palpitations — her Rottweiler Roxanne's behaviour was enough to give anyone palpitations. When Mrs Glover took Roxanne for a walk in her local park the dog found an unexploded hand-grenade and started playing with it. "She was rolling on her back, dropping it and picking it up, coming up to me and pretending to give it to me and then running off again," she said. The more she tried to persuade Roxanne to give up the grenade, the more she thought it was a game. Finally Mrs Glover separated the dog from the bomb: "I wasn't going to touch it, and when I got her to drop it I put her back on her chain and called the police." The live grenade was later packed in sand and blown up by the army, but no one could explain how it ended up in a park.

JANA THE ALSATIAN was taken to the vet suffering from loss of appetite while living near a golf course in Copenhagen. When operated on, she was found to have 13 golf-balls in her stomach. In Sydney, Australia, Earline Graham's Labrador Meatball beat even this record. On his daily walks around the local golf course he managed to scoff 23 balls and had to be operated on to alleviate the severe pain they were causing.

IN NEW YORK, Apple, a nine-month-old border collie, took advantage of her owner Eric Fuch's absence playing bridge to scoff a large chunk of devil's-food cake — and swallowed the foot-long knife he'd left in it as well. The daft dog was rushed to an animal hospital where X-rays revealed the knife in her belly. "Pulling the knife out was the scary thing," said surgeon Elaine Caplan. "It was just amazing the knife didn't slice through the oesophagus." It took two hours to remove the implement, repair internal damage and stitch up the 13-inch cut. Caplan said the dog survived because she swallowed the knife's four-inch handle first instead of the eight-inch blade.

WHEN THE SIMMONS family of Crewekerne, Somerset, returned home from a day on the beach with their springer spaniel, Cass, they became suspicious of a strange noise coming from the animal. "She began rattling," said Ken Simmons, so they took her to the vet. According to vet Robin Carpenter: "When I lifted her onto the table, she sounded like a bag of marbles. In 25 years of practice I have never come across anything like this." Cass was full of pebbles, 31 in all, totalling nearly 2.2lbs (1kg) in weight, some the size of hen's eggs, which she had scoffed surreptitiously during her beach trip. Carpenter removed them and advised the Simmonses to muzzle Cass next time they took her to the seaside.

PEPPER THE POODLE takes the biscuit on the scoffing front – he ate a car. Pepper's owner, Maureen Watkins, left the dog in her Colt Shogun car while she went shopping near her home in Walton-on-Thames. When she returned half-an-hour later she found that the dog had not only chewed his through the Christmas presents, party hats and balloons she had left on the back seat, but had made a meal of the car itself. He had bitten right through the steering wheel, seriously gnawed all the seats and had eaten the head-rests and rubber mats, as well as shredding an AA book and the road maps. Mrs Watkins' husband, Terry, said, "If he hadn't had a cut paw I'm sure he would be on his way to the dog's home." The Watkinses already had an idea of their dog's automotive appetite – the previous year he had ripped the inside out of Mr Watkins' prized BMW. "I should have learned my lesson then," he said. "We repaired the damage and hoped it wouldn't happen again."

IN NEW YORK Flame the Dalmatian developed breathing trouble which persisted for a month, so his owner took him to the vet, where he was given an X-ray. This revealed the cause of the problem – a Bic pen which the dog had somehow snorted and which had become jammed up his nose. The vet yanked the writing implement out with forceps. It was still working.

GUARD DOGS are sometimes more of a liability than an asset, as Andrew Watkins, a pub landlord from Driffield, North Humberside found out to his cost. Feist, his four-year-old German Shepherd ate £1000-worth of notes as his wife Diane was counting the pub's takings. "I couldn't believe it when Feist, who is trained to guard the takings, chewed away at the tenners which were already wrapped up for the bank. We tried to salvage what we could from the remains of the notes, but he had done a very good shredding job and the bank would only accept eight of the notes as genuine legal tender." Their insurance company wouldn't pay out either.

IN CONTRAST, in France a woman's dog guarded her house so well that she had to call the police because it failed to recognise her and wouldn't let her in after she came home with a new hair-do.

NAOMI THE COW had to be rescued by the fire brigade when she got her head stuck in a tree. Naomi, who was pregnant at the time, poked her head into a hollow oak in Laverstock, Hampshire, and couldn't get it out again. When firemen arrived they had to inflate airbags beneath her udder and smear axle grease over her head in order to free her. Fire Chief David Lawrence said, "The poor cow was well and truly stuck. It took us two hours to get her out."

ANOTHER COW had an even luckier escape in Branscombe, Devon. It survived unhurt after falling 100 feet over a cliff and bouncing off a bungalow roof. According to the residents, Charles and Doreen Jordan, on holiday from Haslemere, Surrey: "We thought there had been a landslide, but then we heard a moo." They called the RSPCA after going outside and finding the cow in shock. The Jordans, who had holidayed in the cottage for 30 years, said, "This won't put us off, we love it here."

In Yaoundé, the capital of Cameroon, a bovine from above most definitely put the residents off. In November 1994 a cow from one of the large herds that are led through the city to slaughterhouses every night managed to escape and fell off the cliff above Marguerite Nomo's house. "It was midnight. I was in the living room watching a film – it was *Dances With Wolves* – when I heard a terrible noise. I thought the house was going to collapse," she said. Instead a cow crashed through the roof and shattered the dining table. Firmly convinced black magic was involved, the family moved out. "I am sure this cow was a warning. I can't live here any longer," said Nomo.

EVOLUTION has done the sea otter no favours. It has made it cute and furry, with the endearing trick of floating on its back and using a rock to smash open crustaceans it balances on its chest. However, it has also ensured that this activity dooms the creatures to an early grave. The constant pounding causes the otter's chest to cave in, putting pressure on the heart, resulting in congestive heart disease and premature death.

AT THE UNIVERSITY of Florida Veterinary School, wildlife specialist Dr Elliot Jacobson was presented with a case outside his usual experience – a four-foot pine snake which had swallowed two 15-watt light bulbs. The snake had apparently found them outside a chicken coop near Gainsville and, mistaking them for giant hens' eggs, gobbled them down. The bulbs were removed during an operation, and the snake, nicknamed "G.E." during its stay at the centre, was released three weeks later.

CHARLIE THE CARP exhibited a stunning level of stupidity, even for a fish. Twenty-year-old Charlie (short for Charlotte) lives in fishing ponds at Capesthorpe Hall, near Congleton, Cheshire, and in just two months of the 1994 fishing season, she managed to get caught a record 28 times. It got so bad that the concerned anglers sent her on holiday to a neighbouring pond, but even there she got caught twice. Back in her old pond for the 1995 season, she was caught four times in the first ten days, and would have made it six if she hadn't fallen off the hook twice. Water bailiff Liz Shapley said, "Charlie is the most *stupid* fish I know. She just loves eating, and she's been caught so many times we were worried she might be getting hurt."

FORTEAN TIMES reader Penny Boot wrote in with a story about how her friend Diane was beaten up by a horde of angry squirrels in Chingford Cemetery, north-east London. She was collecting conkers when a pack of squirrels in one of the chestnut trees took to hurling horse chestnuts, still in their spiky shells, at her. They progressed to vigorously shaking branches to make more fall on her. She retreated, suffering eye-watering pain after a particularly large chestnut struck her on the bridge of the nose, leaving her with a massive bruise which made her look as if she'd been in a punch-up.

MEANWHILE on Flinders island, off the southern tip of Australia, grasshoppers were making life difficult for visitors by eating anything coloured green. Tourists were advised against wearing green shirts, as they ran the risk of the insects scoffing them off their backs. They had already eaten green paint, green curtains and even some green underpants left out on a line. "I'm blowed if I know what they want to eat knickers for," said Phill Warren, District Officer for the Department of Agriculture.

The Goat In The Machine

Letting humans loose with machinery is risky
enough — but when animals tangle with
technology, the results can exceed even the
weirdest imaginings

POLAR BEARS on Alaska's Barter Island have been
observed working in teams to wreck the lights on the local
runway. They approach them in a dead straight line and bash
them until they go out. Naturalists are puzzled.

TWO YOUNG bull moose caused £14,000 of damage to
planes at Anchorage International Airport — they banged
their heads against them in an attempt to shed their antlers.

NORTH STAFFORDSHIRE police were driven spare by a pack of feral wallabies loose in the county because they completely wrecked a traffic survey by repeatedly skipping across a road, triggering sensors which were supposed to record cars.

A BAT crashed into an overhead microphone and halted the Northern Ballet Theatre Orchestra's recording of Dracula in All Saints Church, Elland, West Yorkshire.

ROYAL NAVY tenders *Scarab* and *Grassmere* had to have extensive repairs because they were both attacked by metal-eating bacteria. A Navy spokesman said, "We discovered what had happened when the ships started to give off a horrible smell... When we began scraping away the oily sludge, the seawater started to come in." Bacteria which thrive on a mixture of seawater and diesel oil were churning out chemicals which were capable of eroding their way through half-inch steel plate in under three months, and thus peppering the ships with holes.

IN KUWAIT CITY a sheep caused a scene of total chaos by wandering across a busy motorway. Cars swerved in all directions to avoid it, resulting in a 24-vehicle pile-up. The guilty sheep was found nosing curiously among the carnage, unhurt.

BEARS are capable of more directed automotive malice. There is a hoary old urban legend about an escaped circus bear evading hunters by knocking a motorcyclist off his bike and riding away on it, but truth is sometimes almost as strange as fiction. In Russia a bear emerged from the woods to find a motorbike parked by mushroom pickers and, according to *Pravda Severa*, inspected the vehicle and kicked its tyres before mounting. The beast, however, failed to start the bike and, seized by frustration, tore it apart.

DOGS too have made their mark in the biking world. Welsh traffic police were startled when a motorbike hurtled past their car with what looked like an Irish wolfhound wearing a yellow helmet driving it. The police gave chase but failed to get the bike to pull over – instead it swerved into a garage forecourt, bounced across a pavement and then back onto the road, only to crash into the central reservation of a dual carriageway.

When the cops caught up they found David Jones, an oil-rig worker, actually riding the bike, with a pillion passenger behind him and his helmeted pet straddling the tank in front. As for cats and motorbikes, just look at the front of the book!

IF DOGS as bike passengers isn't scary enough, dogs as drivers are downright lethal. Our files bulge with terrifying tales of dogs at the wheel. In 1994 Tessi the cocker spaniel knocked George Haslett's automatic Chevy Blazer into gear and sent the car hurtling 50 yards down Banks Street, Ottawa, fetching up in an antique shop window. Meanwhile Ohio cops managed to chase a careering truck for several miles before finding that the sole occupant, the driver's dog, had put it accidentally into gear.

Elsewhere, Rex the Alsatian also knocked his owner's car into gear and drove the two of them off a cliff in Cumbria. His owner survived, but sadly Rex didn't. In the West Midlands, Evadne Hall had a van crash into her house – with a dog at the wheel. Her husband said, "The dog must have steered the van to get where it was." Police were mystified as to how it released the handbrake.

In the Bronx, New York, another mutt-driven truck injured three people before ramming Max's 99-Cent Store, launching a looting spree; and in Scotland a farmer's wife was killed when her collie sat on her car accelerator, sending it hurtling forward to crush her against a wall.

LEST WE THINK it's only dogs which get the taste for automotive mayhem, it's worth looking at the case of Jamie Eastwood. Eastwood, of South Humberside, was trapped under his digger when driving two pigs for treatment. He had them sitting in his digger cab with him, but when he lifted one pig out of the vehicle the other jumped into the driving seat and nudged the digger into gear, rolling it forward over Eastwood's leg. There's also the case of John Ruppell. Police in Florida stopped his car for erratic driving and were surprised to find a three-foot iguana apparently at the wheel. Ruppell was arrested on a drink-driving charge and the animal was rehoused.

ELECTRICITY and animals have also proved to be a volatile mix. Farmer Walt Walters, of Invernell in Australia, reckoned his chicken Henrietta was a goner when he heard a screeching and clucking from the hen-house and discovered her lying motionless with ruffled feathers and her beak smoking from where she'd stuck it in a power socket. A few minutes later though, she was back on her feet, albeit a little dazed, and seemed none the worse for her ordeal. The next day, however, Mrs Walters dropped one of Henrietta's eggs when collecting them and instead of shattering, it just cracked a little – they were all hard-boiled. "It's the oddest thing that happened in all my years on the farm," said Mrs Walters.

PERCY, thought to be the world's largest pet piranha at a comparatively massive three and a half pounds, came to an appropriate end. He used his razor-sharp teeth to bite through the electrical cable powering the heater in his tank and was instantly fried. Seven other piranha in the tank had a lucky escape and survived.

JAMIE BOUGHTON received a bill for more than £1000 from her garage after she mislaid her pet hamster, Houdini. The creature hid out for two weeks behind the dashboard of her Ford Mondeo where he chewed through all the major electrical cables, wrecking the central locking system and immobilising the engine.

RANDOM POWERCUTS in the village of Lepton, near Huddersfield, had officials from West Yorkshire Electricity baffled, until they saw what Dolly Blue, Billy Whizz and Tommy Sausage were up to. The three shire horses shared a field with a pole supporting the village's electricity cables, and this provided an ideal back-scratcher whenever they suffered a serious itch. When the horses rubbed themselves against the pole they caused it to sway, making the overhead lines touch, and shorting out the village. Local resident Corrina Fillan said, "Who'd have thought a horse's bum would have been responsible?"

WIRES OF A DIFFERENT SORT caused trouble at Chester Zoo. For months the zoo was plagued by phones which rang for no reason, but the mystery was solved when a keeper saw George the Giraffe reach up and wrap his tongue round a phone cable over his enclosure. The phones immediately began ringing, only stopping when George let go – his tongue had shorted the system, setting the bells off.

The zoo raised the cables by three feet, putting them out of George's reach.

A PENSIONER'S DOG was at the root of the opposite problem. She called out engineers as the phone regularly failed to ring when friends called, and when it did the dog always barked first. A technician climbed the phone pole, connected his test rig and dialled the house – no ring. He tried again, the dog barked loudly – the phone rang. British phones signal an incoming call with a 90-volt current sent between two circuits and the ground, triggering the bell. On investigation the technician found the dog was usually tied to the system's ground post, through which the current flowed, with an iron chain and collar. When a call came in the dog got a series of 90-volt shocks, eventually causing it to urinate and bark. The stream of urine would earth the charge and the phone would ring.

DOGS are also pretty good at making phone calls, as well as receiving them. A specially trained Irish setter called Lyric belonging to Judy Bayly saved his asthmatic owner's life by knocking the phone off the hook and dialling the emergency code when her oxygen mask fell off.

Less useful was the call Joan Soper's puppy Ben put through to emergency services. He managed to knock the phone to the floor and dial 112, the new pan-European emergency code. The operator who received the call could only hear barking and occasional heavy breathing, and so sent the police round. They looked through the letterbox and saw a blood-stained phone flung on the floor, so they smashed their way in with sledgehammers, only to find the house empty except for Ben, who was teething – the blood came from his gums.

FOR REAL TROUBLE-MAKING, though, you have to turn to cats. Police in Boynton Beach, Florida, got a silent emergency call on the night of 12 January 1992, traced the call and raced to the address, but got no answer, so they left. An hour later another call came through, followed by several more, so the police returned and woke up the owner, Barbara Maple, who denied making the calls. Investigation revealed it was her cat, possessing the original name of 'Kitten', who had knocked the phone down and dialled 911 – the American emergency code – and then, at various intervals, hit the redial button.

THE INTERNET WORM was a virus-like program which caused widespread havoc a few years ago, but it was a worm of a different sort that crashed Susie Garner's computer's hard drive. Miss Garner, a public relations assistant at Keele University, was baffled by her computer's random shut-downs – until, that is, she looked inside. Wedged inside her hard drive was a live earthworm. Every time it wriggled, the system crashed.

THE SPACE SHUTTLE Discovery had its launch delayed for several weeks in 1995 when NASA found out that two woodpeckers had made 135 holes, each some four inches in diameter, in the fuel tank's insulating foam. The shuttle had to be moved off the launchpad for patching up and the whole operation cost over $100,000. When the craft was finally launched, ground control began the countdown by playing Woody Woodpecker's trademark snicker.

BLACKBIRDS in Guisborough, Cleveland, have learned to mimic car alarms. "I started hearing this irritating noise out-side at 5am every day," said journalist Mark Topping, 32.

"It certainly seemed to be a car alarm, but there wasn't one close enough to be making that sort of row. Then I saw this blackbird sitting outside the bedroom window... it was recreating the din made by a car alarm. After hearing that one I realised others had picked it up as well." Liz Taylor of Melrose, Borders, suggested the birds were enjoying a joke at the expense of their sleeping neighbours. "When I lived in Bombay," she said, "we had a trio of large crows in our garden, one of which could imitate exactly my voice calling for the bearer. When he arrived in response to the summons, they would jump up and down on the wall cackling horribly."

PARROTS, generally the most intelligent of birds, have honed malevolent mimicry to a fine art. One parrot owner had constant trouble with his TV changing channels at random, apparently on its own. Engineers could find nothing wrong with it, so he bought a new set, but the trouble continued. Eventually he realised the trouble only happened when the parrot was in the room. The creature had learnt to mimic precisely the ultrasonic signal from the TV's remote control and was changing channels at will, using ultrasonic sounds inaudible to its owner.

CHAPTER FIVE

On The Rampage

...When animals run riot

ELEPHANTS in the Indian state of Assam have taken to highway robbery. They stop trucks and cars passing through the Garampani wildlife sanctuary and must be bought off with sugar cane or fruit. Most drivers are happy to oblige – Ganesh, the elephant-headed Hindu god, is a symbol of prosperity – but those who refuse to pay the 'toll' risk having their vehicle pushed off the road. Even acquiescing to the pachyderm's pressure has its risks: one truck driver had to have a hand amputated after a large male elephant wrenched a bunch of bananas from his grasp. It all started with drivers throwing sugar cane to baby elephants. Tourists arrived, fruit and cane stalls sprang up, but the carnival atmosphere turned sour as soon as the adult elephants joined in and assumed that receiving tribute was their right. The Assam government responded by posting tame elephants along the road to chase away their wild counterparts. There were plans to ban industrial deforestation and sugar-cane plantations and to discourage further human-elephant contact.

ANOTHER ELEPHANT, whose calf had been knocked down by a locomotive in the Syhelt region of Bangladesh, waited on the line and blocked the next train when it arrived an hour later. She then banged her forehead against the engine for 15 minutes until the engine could no longer run, after which she walked off into the forest, leaving 200 passengers stranded for over five hours.

SIXTY LAMBS were left dead in a field in Germany after a huge flock of crows, numbering in their hundreds, swooped down on them and attacked them. In a scene reminiscent of Hitchcock's celebrated movie, they perched on the lambs' heads and scratched their eyes out.

A CHIHUAHUA-LIKE dog was let out of a motor-home to run around at a petrol station in Valdez, Alaska, while its owners cleaned the windscreen. Suddenly a bald eagle hurtled down from a nearby tree, snatched the dog and flew off towards the harbour with the pooch in its talons.

"It was the damnedest thing I ever saw," said Dennis Fleming, a gas station attendant. "The dog gave one yelp and that was it." The woman owner clutched her hands to her face and cried, "Oh my God!" Fleming said the husband walked around the side of the motor home, out of sight of his wife. Chopping his hands in the air and grinning, he exclaimed, "Yeah! Yeah!"

IN SOUTHERN CHINA more than 2000 frogs fought a pitched battle in a paddy-field in the suburbs of Huitong, with more than 40 of them being killed. A witness said, "The croaking in the paddy-field was deafening as hundreds of frogs rushed to join in the raging battle. Some frogs were fighting individually while others mounted group assaults." It is thought the carnage was sparked off by a mating dispute. The violence ended abruptly after two hours when a boy threw a stone into the field, causing the frogs to flee.

GARY JOHNSON'S visit to a supermarket cost him rather more than he expected – he ended up more than £1000 out of pocket when his dogs ran riot in the car-park. Gary left his dogs tied to a spare shopping trolley outside the supermarket in Cottonwood, Arizona, while he did his shopping. The animals, however, weren't content to sit still. Instead they hurtled off round the car-park, dragging the trolley with them, smashing it into numerous parked cars and leaving their owner with a huge bill for repairs.

NAKED COALMINERS fled in terror when a crazed goat went berserk in their pithead baths at Cadeby Colliery, near Doncaster, Yorkshire. They scattered in all directions to avoid the beast's horns. When the police arrived they found 30 miners outside the building, naked, cold and huddling in a doorway. The cops cornered the goat and took it back to its owner, who claimed children had let it loose

IN SZECHUAN, China, the boot was on the other foot. Shepherds in the region suffered surprising assaults on their flocks of goats from the normally peaceful bamboo-eating pandas of the region. Over a three-year period, pandas ate dozens of goats and even a calf. One family reported being awoken by the barking of their dogs, to find a 220lb (100kg) panda outside, dismembering a sheep that it had apparently killed.

BOTTLE-NOSED DOLPHINS are another reputedly placid and friendly beast whose image has taken a battering in recent years. In the early 1990s, more than 40 small harbour porpoises were found dead on the coast of Scotland's Moray Firth, all killed by massive multiple traumas. Many had their rib-cages crushed and vital organs such as their liver and lungs ruptured. Initially seismic testing, bomb ranges and fishing boats were prime suspects, but then it was found the teeth-marks were those of dolphins, which led to the conclusion that the porpoises had been rammed at high speed by these creatures and killed. Not everyone was convinced, but then a local man, Mike Hancox, filmed the dolphin in the act. "At first I thought the two dolphins were playing with a salmon, but when I looked more closely I could see them flipping up a porpoise with their beaks and battering it when it landed on its back in the water."

A few weeks later a ship's pilot named Norrie Robertson saw four dolphins assassinate another porpoise at the entrance of Cromarty Firth. One rammed the baby porpoise so hard it impaled the infant on its beak. It then shook the half-dead animal free and three other dolphins moved in to finish it off. "It was systematic and organised killing," Robertson said.

EVEN HUMANS are not safe. A Brazilian man died and another was seriously injured when a dolphin rammed them off a beach where swimmers congregate to frolic with the creatures. Joao Moriera, 33, died of internal injuries while 41-year-old Wilson Pedroso suffered broken ribs.

PARK RANGERS in Graves Park, Sheffield were baffled by

the ever growing number of one-legged coots on their lake, until they spotted the culprit – a terrapin. The creature, thought to have been abandoned in the lake by its owner, was snacking on raw drumsticks from the birds as they swam overhead. He was fished out and found a new home. Meanwhile, in Sandusky, Ohio, a fierce giant turtle had to be set free from an aquarium after it killed a shark and savaged two others.

RETIRED BUILDER David Swift found his 200-year-old, 26-room farmhouse under siege from a pair of demented squirrels after he and his wife started feeding the creatures with nuts. Not content with the occasional hand-out, the squirrels moved in, tearing up roof tiles to gain entry and leaving large holes through which the rain poured. Once inside they shredded the roof insulation to make nests, bit chunks out of the beams so that the building needed shoring up, and left several rooms without electricity as they gnawed through the wiring. Then they had babies, so that instead of contending with two squirrels, Mr Swift now had five to get rid of. The last straw came when the chewed-up wiring set bells ringing around the house at all hours, making the Swifts believe the place was haunted. After this, Mr Swift, who is confined to a wheelchair with muscular dystrophy, decided to fight back. He called in taxidermist Don Sharp, who was planning to set traps baited with peanut butter to catch the tiny vandals.

IN DECEMBER 1920 every sheep in Britain went berserk simultaneously. Millions of animals ran amok in complete panic, broke down pens and caused chaos across the country. The same thing happened again in 1938 when sheep simultaneously went crazy in Gloucestershire, Berkshire and

Wiltshire. No explanation for the panics could be found, but one old Berkshire shepherd apparently attributed the 1938 flap to a large flock of geese mistaking the sheep for water in a thick fog and trying to land on them.

AS USUAL, experts were baffled by the fatal stampede which killed 1,000 adult King Penguins and 6,000 chicks found piled four deep in Lusitania Bay on the uninhabited sub-Antarctic island of MacQuarie. Tasmanian conservationist MP Bob Brown was convinced a loud noise or sudden flash of light caused the birds to panic, but government wildlife officials were adamant that no humans had been in the area for weeks. Earthquakes were also ruled out as a cause. Had this happened in the Falkland Islands, it might have been possible to pin the blame on what is reputedly a favoured entertainment of bored Harrier pilots patrolling the coast: penguin toppling. Allegedly when the pilots come across a penguin colony, they catch the birds' attention by flying slowly backwards and forwards in front of them until all the penguins are watching the plane. As they fly left, all the penguins' heads turn left to follow them – back to the right and the penguins turn that way. They do this a few times until the whole colony is behaving like Wimbledon spectators. Then they fly out to sea with the birds still watching, turn the plane round and zoom back directly over the penguins' heads at high speed. All the birds crane upwards to try and follow the rocketing plane – and 10,000 penguins fall flat on their backs.

How Did They Get There?

Animals have an amazing ability to end up in the strangest places... sometimes with hints of teleportation.

CROYDON COUNCIL housing officer Michael Mulligan was dubbed 'The Mousing Director' after he arrived at work with a mouse lodged in his trousers. He was unaware that he had failed to shake it out after it had rushed up his trousers while being chased by a cat at home.

TOSH THE GERBIL also found a unique hiding place — inside a euphonium. It took his 12-year-old owner Liam Malone 17 hours to get him out. The boy spent two hours trying to blow the rodent out, but didn't have enough puff, so his father John, 42, tried to tempt the animal to emerge with titbits, again with no luck. The local vet couldn't shift him either, so they carted the euphonium round to a music shop in Cheltenham, where Tosh was finally released. Shop worker Debbie Sallis explained the delicate procedure: "We were forced to cut through the euphonium tubing, then we greased up the gerbil with washing-up liquid and gave him a shove with a drumstick.... I'm amazed he got out in one piece." John Malone said, "The whole thing drove us round the bend."

IN THE UKRAINE, residents of a village near a natural gas pipeline being built from Siberia to Western Europe were puzzled when they heard a loud roaring coming from inside the partially built pipe, until they found out the cause. A bear had become trapped inside the pipeline and was trying to escape. It eventually ran six miles to the nearest exit where it freed itself – then savagely attacked the pipe.

IN DEBENHAM, Suffolk, firemen received an unconventional call-out... they were asked to free a toad jammed in the spout of a watering can. In 1888 a toad turned up in an even weirder place. Mr Willis of North Farm, Newbury, had a horse which for a long time suffered extreme breathing difficulties, which even an operation by the vet had failed to assuage. As the animal's condition continued to worsen Mr Willis decided to end its suffering and so shot it. Afterwards the corpse was cut up for disposal and, when they severed the neck at the shoulders, a large toad crawled out of the windpipe where it had apparently been jammed, causing the animal's suffering. The toad, which was reddish when extricated, later returned to a more normal colour and was kept by Mr Willis.

CARDIFF SOCIAL WORKER Jean Letton had her Morris 1800 stolen. When it was rediscovered there was a black-and-white rabbit perched contentedly on the back seat. "I have no idea where it came from" said Jean, who is allergic to rabbits. In Birkenhead, meanwhile, a barmaid opening a box of crisps for a customer in the Brittania pub found a hedgehog inside, contentedly scoffing them.

ON THE OTHER SIDE of the world, in Meerut, New Delhi, it took wildlife wardens ten hours to coax a leopard out of a house after the owner returned home to find it asleep on his bed. And in Dhaka, Bangladesh, surgeons fled the operating theatre, leaving the patient behind, when it was invaded by an angry cobra. The snake was beaten to death and the patient lived.

SWEDISH BACKPACKER Magnus Carlstedt, 19 had a 1.5 inch (4cm) cockroach pulled from his ear by ambulancemen using tweezers. It had crawled in there while he slept at the Jolly Swagman hostel in Sydney, Australia. Even more remarkable was the removal of a scorpion from Saleh Awwadh's ear in a Saudi Arabian hospital where he had gone complaining of ear ache. The venomous creature had been lodged firmly in place for at least ten hours – but had not stung Mr Awwadh.

A TEENAGER was stunned when he discovered the cause of the persistent earaches which were preventing him sleeping. Craig Eames, a machinist from Woodville, went to the doctors after suffering constant pain for several days, but never dreamed that the cause was a pregnant spider which had crawled in and become stuck. "I was horrified to think something was crawling around down there," Eames said. "I was told it was pregnant and would have laid its eggs." Doctors removed the creature and Eames made it his pet, carrying it around in a jam-jar. He now sleeps with ear-plugs to prevent it happening again.

THE MUMMIFIED BODY of a 200-year-old mouse was found squashed flat inside an 18th-century hymn-book by a librarian at Salisbury Cathedral, Wiltshire.

SOMETHING VERY LARGE was visiting the first-floor balcony of Holly Craig in the harbour area of Huntingdon Beach in California. On three occasions in two months she found a giant turd lying in the balcony with no evidence as to how it could have got there – no one had seen or heard a thing during the nights when they arrived. Neither the police, the Huntingdon Beach Humane Society or the County Health Department could throw any light on the origin of the substance – which Holly described as "what you might expect from an elephant" – so it was analysed by a vet, who concluded that it was the work of a huge pig. But that still did not explain how a huge pig could sneak onto a first-floor balcony and take a massive dump, unseen, in a built-up area on three separate occasions.

ALSO in Huntingdon Beach, a baby sea lion baffled scientists by turning up at a nursery, where workers discovered it making strange little noises beside a potted pine tree after the area had been flooded by heavy rains. To get there, the animal would have had to swim three miles upstream against ferocious storm currents in the Santa Ana River. Dr Joel Pasco of the Sun and Surf Animal Hospital, where the animal was taken said, "It puzzles the heck out of me how she made it more than three miles up that river. Most of the time the current is too strong for anything to swim against."

SURVEYOR Bjorn Lytskjold was not expecting to come face-to-face with a seal on his mapping expedition in Antarctica – he was in Queen Maud Land, 156 miles from the sea and at an altitude of 396ft, but none the less, that's what he found. It was mummified, staring at him out of the ice like a bizarre Cheshire Cat. "It had a terrible grin. I was really scared," he admitted. A few days later, he found another specimen. No one could figure out how they got so far from the sea, but if it was the result of the movement of the glacier in which they were frozen, they could have been over 100,000 years old. The seals were shipped to the Norwegian Polar Institute in Oslo for further research.

FIVE PENGUINS were found on a small island 100 yards off Genoa, Italy. Authorities were baffled as to how they got there. Likewise, Thai customs were utterly confused when they seized a drifting trawler. There was no one on board, but it contained 100 young kangaroos and various birds.

DOUGLAS AND GLADYS STOWE were at home on the afternoon of 14 August 1982 in the Cape Town suburb of Plumstead when they heard a thump in the lounge. They discovered a beautiful, fat, soot-covered goldfish in their fireplace. Once in a bucket of water, it recovered instantly. Said Mrs Stowe, "It's about twelve centimetres long with a wonderful feathery tail and it's so fat I'm sure it's pregnant." No one in the neighbourhood admitted losing the goldfish, which they believe had been dropped by a crow. Elsewhere, play was stopped during a cricket match at Clifton College, Bristol, when a seagull dropped a mackerel onto the crease.

RETIRED POLICE INSPECTOR Donald MacArthur saw a lamb tumble over 60-foot high cliffs in Dalbeg Bay on the Scottish isle of Lewis. It landed half-way down on a ledge, unhurt, but was out of his reach. He fetched the lamb's owner, crofter George Macleod, but the animal had vanished and they thought it had fallen into the sea. The next day MacArthur saw the animal perched on the summit of Stac-na-Gall, a rock jutting out of the waves 70 feet from the cliff, grazing contentedly. "I couldn't believe it," he said. "Locals said he could have been swept off the ledge by a powerful golden eagle before the bird realised he was too heavy and dropped him. The other explanation is that he jumped down at low tide and crossed a sandbank. But no one can figure out how he scrambled up the sheer sides of the stack. If that was the case, he must have the mountaineering ability of Sherpa Tensing." The lamb, now named Tensing, spent two weeks as a tourist attraction until he fell half-way down the rock. He was rescued by Inspector Calum Watt from the Scottish Society for the Prevention of Cruelty to Animals. "The sheep's fine," he said, "apart from grazed shins. If he hadn't slipped down the stack I don't know if we would have ever got him down."

THERE IS a whiff of urban legend in this tale, but it originates from the church magazine of St John with St Michael in Bournemouth, Dorset. Apparently, the vicar's cat got stuck up a tree and, unable to reach it with a ladder, he devised a scheme to bring it down another way. He threw a rope over the bough on which the cat was stuck, attached the other end to his car bumper, then drove away slowly, thus lowering the bough so that the cat could jump down. Unfortunately, part-way down the rope snapped, rocketing the unfortunate moggy skywards. Meanwhile, a mother and daughter were picnicking on a lawn nearby. "Mummy, I'd like to have a cat," said the girl. "You'll have to ask Jesus for one," said Mum, at which point the flying feline came hurtling through the air and landed on their lawn. It has stayed with them ever since.

A FOUR-YEAR-OLD cat named Bruno survived 45 days trapped under the floorboards of a house being renovated two doors from his home in Teignmouth. Bruno, who weighed more than 16lbs (7kg) when he disappeared, was discovered in an emaciated state after builder Derek Snell heard faint cries while working on the property. Bruno had probably crawled under floorboards, which were then nailed back into place. His owners Aubrey Pitts and Merrill Colbourne had given up hope of ever seeing him again. When they got him back Mr Pitts said, "The poor thing was like a sack of bones with a head. We rushed him to the vet, who checked his breathing and his heart and that was all right, but he suffered temporary blindness through the shock and the vet initially thought he must have had a stroke.... I cannot believe he lasted so long without any water."

DAVID AND BRENDA POWELL thought they had the same problem in their three-bedroom house in Lydney, Gloucestershire, when they heard mewing from inside the bathroom walls. The couple contacted the RSPCA, the fire brigade and the Cat Protection League, but failed to find the source of the sound. When the mewing began to drift through plugholes and echo down the pipework, Carla Lane, the TV script writer and animal obsessive, called in International Rescue, who are normally summoned to major natural disasters. They spent 14 hours searching the house, all but demolishing it in the process. They used thermal imaging cameras, dismantled the lavatory, removed the bath, knocked holes in the hall and bathroom walls and lifted floorboards, but found nothing. Various hypotheses were suggested: the cat had its own access to the wall cavity; it was frightened to death by the sounds of the search; or that there never was a cat in the first place. Whatever the truth, the abuse they received from animal lovers for not finding the animal forced the Powells to flee to Belgium.

WHEN MISSA the cat was ready to give birth in Alesund, Norway, her owners were on holiday, so she found her own place to produce kittens – in a vacant magpie nest. When her owners, the Muren family, came home, they were bemused to hear mewing coming from a tree in the garden.

US CUSTOMS officers in Texas searching a pick-up truck as it crossed the Mexican border made a surprising find – six live snakes hidden in a tool compartment behind the driver's seat, which, although rare, was not unprecedented. What they found when they searched the two men in the vehicle was a bit more unusual: eight more snakes wrapped in socks and pantyhose, hidden in the men's underwear. Customs officer Humberto Rodriguez said, "In the past we have found marijuana and other drugs in groin areas, but never snakes in jockey shorts." Mark Johnson, a Fish and Wildlife Service officer, commented: "They are pretty docile, but I wouldn't want to have them in my pants." Someone who clearly did, though, was Brian Dawson of Cleveland, Ohio. He was arrested for speeding and driving on a falsified licence, and while changing into jail uniform he surprised police when a boa constrictor popped its head out of his boxer shorts. Dawson claimed he'd put it there to keep it warm.

Rescued

Dolphins are famous for rescuing shipwrecked sailors, but they are not the only creatures to turn Samaritan.

THE CREW of a coastal steamer wrecked off Sydney in 1898 were saved by their cargo of pigs. The captain tied life-lines to the pigs and threw the creatures overboard. They quickly swam ashore, taking the lines with them, and thus providing an escape route for everyone on board.

A PIG also came to the rescue of farmer Liu Ming-Hui in Taiwan. He was taking his favourite boar to stud when he was knocked senseless by a car. The pig ran home, got Liu's wife to follow him and took her to where Liu was lying injured in the road.

BITSY THE SCHNAUZER saved her owner Jesus Martinez, 60, when he had a heart attack at the wheel of his car on a motorway in Houston, Texas, by leaping into the driver's seat and knocking the wheel to force the car onto the hard shoulder. She then bit Martinez until he took his foot off the accelerator. The car stopped safely and Martinez recovered in hospital.

DOGS HAVE ALWAYS been adept at retrieving, but Bruce the Labrador is particularly expert at finding cricket balls, a skill which his owner has put to use in the service of several Durham cricket clubs. Mr Morales, Bruce's owner, has kept a record of his dog's finds, which now top 500, the 500th being from a cemetery at Sacriston.

IN NORFOLK, Brian Simons from King's Lynn got a surprise when he threw a stick into the River Nar for his dog Laddie to retrieve. The dog ignored the stick and instead came back with a 12-pound pike in his mouth. Brian, who returned the flapping fish to the water, said, "I've been fishing for 27 years and I've never seen anything like it.... Who needs a fishing rod when you've got a dog like Laddie?"

A DIFFERENT LADDIE, this time from Wickham Market, Suffolk, saved his owner's life. He was in the garden with 17-year-old Tom Clements when he started pawing the ground, then ran to the house. Puzzled, Tom followed him, and a moment later a 120ft beech tree crashed down on the spot where they had been playing. Tom believed the dog's acute hearing had allowed him to pick up the sound of roots snapping underground in the 45mph winds, alerting him to the tree's imminent collapse.

ANOTHER LIFESAVER was Bonita Whitfield's Dobermann/collie cross, Baby, which discovered a malignant tumour on her owner's thigh and tried to bite it off. The dog ignored other moles and marks on the woman's body, but spent several minutes a day sniffing the tumour. The respected medical journal *The Lancet* said that the dog "may have saved her owner's life" by prompting her to seek treatment while the lesion was still curable.

FRIENDLY, an Alsatian living in a rural district north-west of Chicago, was too late to save any lives — but did succeed where the police failed. She dragged home first one, then a second decomposing human leg, to her owner's horror. They called the police who identified the legs as from the same body, believed to be a white woman aged between 16 and 25. They combed the district for the rest of the corpse, but, unlike Friendly, they could find no trace of it.

IN DECEMBER 1976 Lew Foley was driving across the Yorkshire Moors with his nine-month-old pet lion Cassius when he stopped to let the animal out for some exercise. The animal immediately ran off into the darkness, with Foley and his brother Harry in pursuit. The chase took them across bleak Langsett Moor near Sheffield until they caught up with the lion, who was standing over a body of a woman lying unconscious in the snow. Cassius had been drawn by the woman's scent, and had found her unconscious and clad in flimsy indoor clothing in freezing temperatures. The brothers wrapped her in warm clothing and took her to

Deepcar police station, where she was transferred to Sheffield Royal Hospital, suffering from exposure and exhaustion. She had left Middlewood Psychiatric Hospital and walked sixteen miles across the moor. If Cassius had not found her she wouldn't have survived the night.

SMALLER CATS, too, have made their share of rescues. In Beijing a cat called Ugly Sister saved a family from a collapsing mud house by pushing open the window and pulling urgently on her owner's trousers. Li-Shuhua noticed that mud was starting to fall from the wall of the house and rushed his family outside. They got out seconds before the building caved in.

SIERRA, a seven-month-old Alsatian cross, saved her Labrador playmate Bowdie, who fell 30 feet into an abandoned well in Oak View, California. She stood by the well howling until firefighters arrived to lift the fallen dog out. In Sweden, it was deer which alerted searchers looking for 23-year-old Ollie Hedin, who had gone missing after setting out alone to go rock climbing. After hours of searching Leif Haglund noticed a group of deer standing by a huge rock, and was surprised that they showed no sign of fleeing at his approach – they stood still, staring at something on the ground, and did not bolt until he was almost close enough to touch them. When he got to where the deer had been, he saw what they had been staring at – it was Ollie Hedin, trapped and unconscious at the bottom of a narrow, overgrown crevice where he had been for three days. If it wasn't for the deer he would never have been found.

WHEN LISA NELSON, 20, slipped from a rain-slick trail and fell more than 75 feet into a gorge in Ithica, New York

State, her life was saved by a raccoon. This one didn't raise any alarms or alert any rescuers, though – Ms Nelson landed on it, cushioning her impact. Rescuers found the woman and the raccoon lying side by side at the bottom of the gorge. Ms Nelson was treated in hospital for a broken wrist and minor injuries, while the raccoon received treatment at an animal shelter.

IN THE CZECH town of Domazlice a stray dog urinated on a semtex bomb left in a shop doorway, and saved the lives of five people. The pee-soaked hammer kept the bomb from exploding.

FELLENE, a chihuahua belonging to Tammy Dalton of Salt Lake City, Utah, suckled two stray kittens which her owner brought home. Even Fellene's six-week-old puppy Champ accepted them. And in Florida, Tiny, a four-year-old chihuahua raised a kitten named Tiger, which her owners, Craig and Tim Lawson, had found abandoned on Vero Beach.

IN NEW ZEALAND it was a rabbit which got the benefit of a canine foster parent. Tisha, a 14-year-old King Charles spaniel unearthed a litter of five orphaned baby rabbits and brought them back to the farm where she lived, producing milk to feed them. This was all the more extraordinary as she usually enthusiastically devoured any rabbits she caught.

A BABY RABBIT in Warwickshire had a narrow escape on the Forest of Arden golf course. Jeremy Blyth and three companions were walking towards the tenth green when they heard a commotion in the bushes and the rabbit rushed out with a stoat in hot pursuit. Just beyond the green the stoat leapt on the squealing rabbit and that looked to be the end of that — but they were wrong. The row had attracted the attention of twenty Canada geese who advanced on the stoat, hissing and waving their necks menacingly. The stoat dropped the rabbit and darted back into the bushes, and the geese formed a protective circle round the frightened animal until it hopped away into the long grass. Seeing its opportunity the stoat started after the rabbit again, only to be headed off by a line of hissing birds. This was repeated several times until the rabbit reached permanent safety. Natural History Museum bird expert Peter Colston said, "I have never heard of anything like this before!"

LOTTIE STEPHENS, 18, and a friend were on a fishing trip near the Pacific island of Vanuatu when their boat capsized on 15 January 1990. His friend died, and after four days Lottie decided to swim for it. He claimed he was saved by a sting-ray which carried him 450 miles over 13 days despite shark attacks. He was washed up on the shores of New Caledonia on 7 February.

A TURTLE saved Korean sailor Lim Kang-Yong, 28, after he fell overboard from his ship, the *May Star*, in the Bay of Bengal. He grabbed the passing reptile and clung to it until spotted by his crew-mates six hours later. They used a crane to pull him and the three-foot turtle from the sea. "The turtle was very friendly and did not hurt me at all," said Mr Lim. After a meal of meat and bananas, the turtle was returned to the sea.

Swarm!

Plagues of locusts are famed for their destructive powers, but all sorts of other creatures gather into vast hordes – with unpredictable results.

VILLAGERS in Sestroretsky on the coast of Kamchatka, Russia, were amazed when a vast army of white Arctic hares marched straight through the centre of their village in tight formation, ignoring the barking dogs that ran along their flanks. The thousand-strong army headed unerringly towards the beach where they scoffed washed-up sea kale as though they were starving, topping their meal off with a seven-acre field of cabbages. The hares then reformed their ranks and headed back through the village in the same orderly fashion, before dispersing into the frozen wilderness. Experts were baffled by the behaviour, although one possible explanation is that the hares were suffering from a mineral imbalance which the mineral-rich kale corrected.

IN A POSITIVELY biblical scenario, priest Antonio Razzini fought a losing battle against a plague of snakes that was infesting his church in Pavia, Italy. "No one listens to the services any more. All they think of is how to fend off these wretched serpents – some are three feet long," moaned the besieged priest.

THE BODY of a 98-year-old woman lay unburied for hours after 200 mourners fled her funeral after being attacked by a vast swarm of angry bees in Malawi. In Sierra Leone, a different kind of ritual attracted attention from bees – a female circumcision ceremony. A huge swarm descended on the event, stinging indiscriminately and putting half of the 100 participants in hospital before the ritual could begin, saving many girls from mutilation.

THE PICTURESQUE village of Branscombe, Devon, appealed to the Ministry of Agriculture for help after being besieged by a horde of badgers. Locals claimed the badgers were ransacking gardens, attacking chickens, ruining lawns, overturning dustbins and blocking traffic in the narrow lanes around the village. There were an estimated 400 badgers in the colony, outnumbering the 370 villagers. Parish Council spokesman Jim Reddaway said, "Some villagers find them on the doorstep in the morning when they go to collect their milk. It won't be long before they're taking over our homes."

WHEN FARMER Bill Langford found three of his cows lying dead in a salt marsh where they grazed, he was mystified as to what could have killed them, so he had an autopsy carried out on the bodies. He was amazed at what was found. The cattle had suffocated – on mosquitoes. The animals' lungs were full of fluid and their bodies were "pretty devoid of blood" but the clincher was that their nostrils were found to be crammed with the insects' tiny corpses. Randall theorised that the cows had been weakened by blood-loss caused by massive numbers of mosquito bites, but finally suffocated from trying to breathe the mosquito-thick air.

WEAPONS which went missing and were used in coup attempts against the president of the Phillippines, Cory Aquino, cannot be recovered because swarms of termites have eaten all the records about them. At least, that's what the investigating tribunal was told.

A HUGE FLOCK of jackdaws has been terrorising the western Romanian town of Turda, attacking inhabitants, especially children, "going so far as to steal the fruit they are holding" according to the private TV channel Pro-TV. "We do not dare go out in the park with our children," said one mother.

A FLOCK of several hundred black-and-white birds hurtled down the chimney of Chris Thomas's house in Port Angeles, Washington State, bursting through the glass fireplace cover with a roar and wrecking the living room. They scattered soot and ash all over the place and, according to Thomas, most, if not all, the birds relieved themselves in the house, adding to the mess. "You cannot imagine what hundreds and hundreds of loose birds can do in your house," she said. The family called the fire brigade, who evicted the birds with their hands, feet, brooms and other implements. However, once freed, the birds circled the house a few times, then plunged back down the chimney again. Firemen had to cover the top to prevent the invasion continuing.

SALT-WATER CRABS were spotted crawling from the freshwater drainage system of Newport, near Launceston. Cornwall. RSPCA inspector Nigel Thomas was called in and removed several from the town's storm drains, but a few days later many more live crabs and nearly two dozen dead ones were discovered in the road nearby. The live crabs were returned to the sea, but 'experts' were puzzled as to how so many live crabs had been found so far inland – Launceston is fifteen miles from the sea.

EVERY SPRING Lufkin, Texas, is invaded by an immense horde of crawfish – nocturnal land-based relatives of the lobster. On spring nights they swarm out of their holes, in which they hibernate for most of the year, and begin to mate. The females then build hollow mounds of clay about 18 inches high, which soon fill with rainwater. The Texas sun bakes the mounds rock-hard and the landscape becomes scattered with the huge solid lumps, which make farming almost impossible. Not only do farmers have to cope with a creeping crustacean carpet, but they suffer constant damage to their tilling and mowing equipment from the hard mounds, resulting in inadequately tended crops producing poor yields. All pesticides have proved ineffective against the crawfish and farmers have resorted to pouring crushed mothballs, carbide or burning oil down their holes to fight back. Even so the crawfish keep coming. The worst hit area near Lufkin had over 27,000 crawfish mounds per acre, and in Angelina county some 200,000 acres are affected. "It's like a horror movie," said Hal Brockman, district conservationist for the US Department of Agriculture.

CHINESE MITTEN CRABS posed a major threat to river safety along the rivers Ouse and Wharfe in Yorkshire. The mitten, named for its hairy pincers, became established in Europe in the 1930s and first appeared in Yorkshire in 1986. Its habit of burrowing deep into clay threatened to undermine new flood defences along the rivers. "Frankly, this is an eventuality for which we had not planned," a National Rivers Authority spokesman said.

A DAM near the site of the legendary Queen of Sheba's Great Dam of Marib was threatened by an invasion of mice in 1993. The Modern Dam was built in the early 1980s to restore prosperity to a remote part of the Yemen, which had been neglected since the fall of the kingdom of Saba (the Arabic name for Sheba) and the subsequent collapse of the original dam. Yemeni legend has it that the Great Dam's foundations were undermined by a plague of mice before its final collapse in a flood in AD579.

IN 1980 Australia suffered a massive plague of mice. The plague began the previous year, but by April 1980 100,000 square miles had been affected by the starving horde, with the creatures reported as eating everything from putty to wedding dresses. Some desperate householders tried to fend them off with barricades of soap-impregnated steel wool (Brillo pads!) which proved utterly ineffective. Even water wouldn't stop them – one family reported the rodents swimming out to their yacht. Mr Barbary, a resident of one of the affected towns, Woomelang, said, "Poison is useless. After a while they eat it like cheese."

A HORDE of tortoises mysteriously appeared on Hainault Forest golf course in 1979.

HAMELIN, the German town famed for the legend of the Pied Piper, was being overrun by rats once again in 1991. Thousands were breeding in the drains, town hall and surrounding fields, and were swarming all over the town.

A NUCLEAR PLANT in Dava Bay, Shenzen, China was under siege from termites. The insects, which had already eaten huge quantities of bank notes in an unnamed Shenzen bank, laid siege to the power plant attacking buildings and wiring as well as invading the city reservoir, closing an electronics factory by eating its power cables and blacking out a local hotel by the same means.

Sex Beasts

In the popular imagination 'animal sexuality' implies an energetic and undiscriminating sex drive. Taking a look at these stories suggests that's not far off the mark.

FISHERMAN Michael Armstrong hooked a 180lb skate at Clew Bay, County Mayo, Ireland and spent an hour and a half trying to land it. When he did he found out the reason for the lengthy struggle – his catch was in the middle of mating with a female. Unperturbed by its capture, the fish continued to mate enthusiastically in the bottom of the boat, much to Armstrong's amazement.

A MARINE MATING of an even stranger kind took place off the coast of Norway in 1994. A thirteen-foot killer whale spent ten days courting the *Voksa*, a 150-foot car ferry. The whale, which appeared to have become separated from her pod, hugged the side of the ferry as it travelled from village to village among the islands off the Norwegian coast. Kjell Nystoeyl, the *Voksa*'s skipper, said, "There must be some vibration from the ship's hull that she finds comforting."

TWENTY OVERSEXED BULLS escaped from their farm in Kolsva, Sweden, and surrounded a police car as it was taking a drunk to the lock-up. One bull mounted the bonnet while others rubbed themselves sensuously against the doors or caressed the boot. "Under the circumstances, we did not find it urgent to leave the our car until the rutting horde was distracted by a lorry," said one of the constables.

ANOTHER RANDY BULL caused chaos in Bombay by spending two hours energetically mating with a cow on the airport runway. As cows are sacred animals there it was not possible to shoo them out the way, and 26 flights were delayed until the amorous interlude ended.

COWS in New Zealand were less fortunate. An entire herd on a dairy farm in Auckland stopped producing milk as a result of stress caused by a confused elephant seal trying to mate with them. The 6,000-pound seal destroyed gates and fences trying to reach the cows, and poked a hole in a 10,000-gallon water tank while trying to make love to it.

HEROICALLY DOOMED couplings with inanimate objects aren't just the province of seals. Chi-Chi, a Vietnamese pot-bellied pig from Florida, faced castration after he raped a Harley Davidson motorbike, scratching paint and tearing the seat fabric, while in Nebraska a prairie chicken turned up on J. B. Fischer's ranch and immediately began performing its courtship ritual to the farmer's pickup truck, inflating its airsacs and making a booming noise which could be heard a mile away. In Kalmar, Sweden, a bat took a fancy to a computer in an electronics workshop, repeatedly returning to cling to the console. Technicians thought it had been seduced by the high-pitched squeal the machine produced on overload, which is similar to a bat's mating call. In Montana, it was a brush that proved to be irresistible: Prickles the porcupine moved into the shed of farmer Sid Toomey and refused to leave, turning his amorous attentions to a broom stored there. "He just worships the damn thing," said Sid.

MORE FLAMBOYANTLY, a rhino in the Central African Republic caused a stir by enthusiastically humping a full-size model dinosaur outside the national museum in Bangui. The model, worth over £20,000, was damaged beyond repair and the rhino was captured and returned to its native habitat. Once there though, it might have found the tables turned. On a nature reserve in Pilansberg, South Africa, a group of orphan male elephants have been causing havoc due to the absence of control from their elders. As well as attacking tourists and game wardens, they have taken to raping rhinos in the park.

MARINE BIOLOGIST Richard Lutz got a surprise when studying clams from the mini-submarine Alvin on a lava bed 8,000 feet under the ocean surface. He videotaped two octopuses mating, thus inadvertently creating the first inter-species gay porn video. Janet Voight of Chicago's Field Museum of Natural History, who was called in to study the tape, made some interesting discoveries. Both octopuses had a specialised arm characteristic of males and used for sexual purposes, and that they were of two different species. In the video the smaller octopus, a white species unknown to science, was sitting on top of an unidentified brown one and was rubbing its sexual arm along its partner's back. It then reached under the larger male and inserted the tip of its arm into the other's body cavity. The white octopus's body then began to expand and contract rapidly, which signifies mating. Although captive octopuses occasionally indulge in homosexual behaviour, it had never been observed in the wild before. Voight suggested that maybe the shortage of suitable mates in the deep ocean compels octopuses to indulge in indiscriminate coupling on the off-chance of reproduction, but admitted to being generally baffled by the whole performance.

IN TAIWAN it's the giraffes which are getting confused. The three males in Taipei zoo turned to homosexuality after their female companion died, repeatedly mounting each other. The zoo resorted to importing a new female because embarrassed keepers were running out of explanations for children viewing the spectacle. Meanwhile, dubious research from a Turkish university in 1981 claimed that disco music drove mice to homosexuality, and would probably do the same to humans.

IT WAS DIET that caused sexual confusion among Australian sheep in 1994. Research by the Commonwealth Scientific and Industrial Organisation in Perth found that female sheep were behaving like males and trying to mount their rams because there had been a dry winter, during which many sheep had been undernourished, followed by a wet spring, producing plentiful lush grass. The sudden increase in nutrients apparently put the sheep into shock and scrambled electrical signals in the brain, producing masculine behaviour.

RESEARCH at Carroll College in Helena, Montana, has thrown further light on sheep sexuality. Investigations by animal behaviourist Anne Perkins have revealed that up to ten per cent of rams are homosexual, and that the condition has a genetic origin. "It's been known that some rams don't breed," she said, "and we wanted to find out why. It used to be thought they were just shy but when we took them away from the ewes and put them back among other rams we found out a lot of them weren't shy: they were male-orientated. They started enthusiastically-mounting other rams. They were attempting rectal entry, and occasionally the other ram would co-operate and they would achieve it." Postmortem examination of the rams' brains revealed a low level of activity in the preoptic area, which is known to have a role in sexual behaviour. They also had higher levels of an oestrogen-like chemical called estradiol in their brains.

Lesbianism in sheep, though, is a lot harder to fathom as Anne Perkins – we think it's the same researcher, although this report came from the University of California – discovered. One of her findings was that "it is very difficult to look at the possibility of lesbian sheep because if you are a female sheep, what you do to solicit sex is to stand still. Maybe there is a female sheep out there really wanting another female, but there's no way for us to know it."

IT IS UNLIKELY that sheep-to-sheep mating was responsible for an incident which took place in Torquay in 1993. Police spent most of an evening pursuing a stray sheep through the town, only this was a sheep with a difference –

it was wearing a bra and panties. PC Tim Eden said, "I've heard of mutton dressed as lamb and sheep in wolf's clothing – but a ewe in undies?" He clearly had not seen Woody Allen's film *All You Ever Wanted to Know About Sex But Were Afraid to Ask*, in which Gene Wilder is caught *in flagrante delicto* with a similarly clad sheep.

AND IT ISN'T just on the screen that stars experience unfortunate sexual encounters with the animal kingdom. Johnny Depp suffered a traumatic interlude in a hotel in America's deep south while trying to make love to his girlfriend – he was attacked by an armadillo which hurled itself on his back. Depp explained, "I was putting on a condom when it jumped out of a closet." At least he escaped unscathed, which is more than can be said for Zsa Zsa Gabor's husband, Prince Frederick von Anhalt. He was fast asleep when Gabor's pet terrier leapt on him and sank its teeth into his penis, refusing to let go until the Prince thumped it. The Prince was rushed to a nearby clinic where the mangled organ was stitched up, and he was told he would make a full recovery.

WHILE DOGS might be expected to do this sort of thing, they are not the only creatures who do. A 27 year-old Malaysian man had his penis bitten completely off by a tortoise after taking a dip in a pool near Batu Arang. He searched the water fruitlessly for the severed member before seeking medical help.

HENRY KISSINGER may have had a reputation as a bit of a playboy in his prime, but there is little about him which exudes obvious sexual allure – unless, that is, you are a frog. When Kissinger spoke at Bohemia Grove in California, the resident frogs went berserk, causing such a racket that a herpetologist was called in to investigate. He taped Kissinger's voice and played it back to the frogs, and they immediately went wild again. It seems the former diplomat's baritone voice resembles that of a male frog in heat, stimulating all the females in the area to answer back. This may sound weird, but frogs and toads are pretty indiscriminate in their mating behaviour. Giant Hungarian Marsh Frogs, breeding at Romney in Kent, create a constant din by returning mating calls to passing tractors, planes and motorbikes. Toads wreaked havoc among Ken Pearson's koi carp in Leyland, Lancashire. He kept finding dead fish in his pond but was baffled as to what was killing them, until one morning he found a fish floating with a toad clamped firmly to it. It turned out that, although much smaller than the fish, toads were trying to mate with his prized carp, holding them in a vice-like grip until they suffocated and died.

THIS SORT OF THING was proposed by a Norwegian university lecturer to account for the death of eighteen cows near the provincial town of Sebu. He reckoned they had all been raped and killed by a randy bear. The news created a world-wide stir. Within hours an equal and opposite expert from the Oslo Biology Institute was wheeled out to say the whole idea was ridiculous, leaving everyone none the wiser as to what had screwed eighteen cows to death.

LUMBERJACK Peter King was also accused of killing the object of his affections with over-enthusiastic lust. He was arrested on animal cruelty charges after he caught rabies from a raccoon he had sex with, which his accusers claim led to its death. King refuted the charge. He said the raccoon was already dead when he molested it.

ANOTHER SURPRISING COUPLING took place in Key West, Florida, in 1993. Canella the Rottweiler was lying tied up on Kevin Foley's patio while he went indoors to get her some food. As he did so, Rocky the chihuahua moved in and started mating furiously with the prone bitch. A passing animal control officer, amazed by the spectacle, hosed the odd couple apart while Foley took a photograph. A month later Canella was found to be pregnant, but the litter had to be aborted by hysterectomy, leaving the dog sterile. Foley then sued Rocky's owner, Dayami Diaz, for $2,567.50 to compensate for the loss of his dog's breeding potential.

DOGS' BASIC INSTINCTS also got the better of them at Winsford in Somerset, when the all-male East Dulverston pack of foxhounds picked up the scent of 30 broody bitches from the Exmoor hunt. The fox was forgotten and a massive canine orgy ensued, which took huntsmen an hour and a half to break up.

Almost Human

Humans like to assume they are unique – but the behaviour of some of these creatures may make you think again.

SEAGULLS in the Top Valley area of Nottingham have been found smashing the covers on streetlamps – and then sitting on the naked bulbs to keep themselves warm.

IN SOUTHSEA, Hampshire, an octopus caused a stir when it learned to unscrew jar lids and feed itself. Staff named him Einstein.

BIRD LOVER Anders Turesson had a pet crow with a particularly useful talent. It was trained to pick up his dirty clothes, fly them to the washing machine and switch it on at his home in Stockholm, Sweden.

SHEEP on Isobel McIntosh's farm in Aberdeenshire showed an uncharacteristic turn of intelligence when it came to escaping from their field. Two ewes and their lambs continually managed to get out, no matter how well they seemed to be fenced in. Mrs McIntosh and her husband were baffled until a neighbour tipped them off to the sheeps' ruse. They would wander round, prodding the fence until they found a weak spot. One ewe would then butt it until she could get her head through, then the other would rush at her from behind and butt her extremely hard so that she shot right through, leaving an opening large enough for the rest of the adventurous sheep to make their escape.

ANOTHER CREATURE with a penchant for slipping through fences was Wofford the golden retriever, who sneaked through a gap in his garden fence and into the branch library next door, where he picked up a childrens' book and waited patiently in line with it. The librarian took the book and gave him a few chew toys to play with, but within minutes Wofford was back browsing. Unable to reach his owner, David Viccellios, the library called Animal Control which came and collected him, later serving a summons on Mr Viccellio under 'Dog at Large' laws, forcing him to make an appearance in court. "That's pretty steep for just going to the library," he complained. Apparently Wofford had always been a book-hound, taking books to bed when a pup, and he usually greeted visitors by offering them a book from the coffee table. Mrs Viccellio said, "I don't know where he got so interested in books. He's a retriever, but he's never the least bit interested in retrieving.

Throw a stick or a ball and he just goes over and lays down next to it. But books get him excited."

AN ALSATIAN in Seville also fell foul of the law in March 1996. It was nabbed as a handbag thief after dragging a woman to the ground and trying to make off with her purse. By August that year it appeared to have relocated to New York, as police there began receiving reports of a dog picking pockets in Central Park.

CATS, TOO, can have a larcenous turn, often specialising in particular items. Sammy, who belonged to Hilda Greyson of Saltash, Cornwall, had a taste for men's socks, bringing home fourteen pairs and six assorted odd ones. Mrs Greyson had no idea where they came from and even went to the trouble of advertising in the local paper to find their owners, but to no avail.

For Fujji the Siamese cat, it was paintbrushes that got him going. His owner, Judy Ferris of Cleeve, near Bristol, was sitting in the garden when Fujji arrived with the first one, a four-inch brush. Half an hour later he was back with a seven-inch one, and since then has brought home seven more. Mrs Ferris said, "We have no idea who they belong to. They're worth quite a lot."

Suki, a three-year-old black-and-white cat from Croydon, had more catholic tastes. She would bring home all sorts of clothes – one day a blouse and a petticoat, then four jumpers, and all sorts of other items. Like the previous cat owners, Mrs Weatherspoon, Suki's owner, was unable to trace the source of the garments. "I think all the clothes come from one person because they are always clean but a little damp, as though someone had them in a basket ready to hang on the line."

THE KING of feline thieves, though, has to be Blackie, of Much Wenlock in Shropshire. Starting by collecting sweet wrappers and crisp packets, Blackie developed impressive kleptomania and towed home odd shoes, gloves – especially gardening gloves, of which he stole six pairs – socks, towels, sponges, blouses, pan scrubbers, table napkins and shirts. He became so notorious in the town that when items went missing, people would always check with Audrey Williamson, Blackie's owner, to see if she had them. "Only this morning I returned a pair of blue leather shoes to a lady who had been advised to pay me a visit," said Mrs Williamson.

CATS ARE NOT exclusively wedded to the criminal; some are paragons of virtue. One such creature is Bramble, who lives in the churchyard of St Mary's Church, Attenborough, Nottingham, and attends every service held in the church, usually sitting on someone's lap.

She shows extreme determination in attending sevices, and at one memorial service she rushed in late, squeezing in through a partly open door. During sermons she moves to the front and sits absolutely still in front of the lectern until the vicar has finished. For her dedication, the cat has been rewarded with her own comic strip in the parish magazine.

IN KUALA LUMPUR, Thailand, another religious cat went even further. She strolled into a Buddhist temple and drew attention to herself by apparently praying. The cat sat up on her hind legs, put her forepaws together and moved them up and down quickly, rather as human worshippers do. Sri Dhammananda, the priest in charge of the temple, said, "Its behaviour is a projection of the habits of its previous birth. Because of karma, rebirth took place in the animal kingdom." Meanwhile, in Taiwan, a tiger which was about to be slaughtered so that its meat could be sold as a magic aphrodisiac was saved by a bunch of Chinese priests who paid £5000 for it. They claimed to have "converted it to Buddhism" and sent it to Kaohsiung Zoo.

THE CALL OF RELIGION may be irresistible to some animals, but more base human inventions, such as television, obsess others. In Beausejour, Canada, teenager Joshua Fosty got the surprise of his life when he went to the family's basement den to watch TV — his place was already taken by a bear which was sprawled in front of the TV, next to the fireplace, munching potato crisps. Joshua stepped towards the beast and it struck out at him, swiping him with his claws, and causing him to flee to his parents in terror. They didn't believe him at first, but when they saw the clawmarks they called the police, who raced to the scene and shot the ursine couch potato dead.

AND BEARS are just the tip of the iceberg. In Evesham, Worcestershire, animal rescue workers were called out by a shocked family who found a ferret cheerfully viewing the telly from their sofa, while in the Chinese province of Jiangxi an owl likes TV so much that it has built its nest in a farmer's house so it can watch the box every day. It arrived in April 1992, perched on a beam and started watching, but now it sleeps under the eaves during the day and watches telly from the dinner table all night.

IN AN ANIMAL HOSPITAL near Litchfield, Staffordshire, the only thing that will calm Dylan, the hyperactive raccoon, is *Coronation Street*. He tears round the place constantly, sticking his nose in everything, except when the soap opera is on. His special favourite was the Rover's Return land-lady, Bet Gilroy, played by actress Julie Goodyear. "He just sits there gooey-eyed when she is on the screen," said Rob Smith who runs the animal sanctuary. "We've taped several episodes... and when we want a bit of peace and quiet we play a video tape."

SHEBA, an alsatian/collie cross owned by Ann McLane from Middlesbrough lived up to her Lassie-like ancestry when her owner locked herself out of her car, leaving the dog inside with her handbag. After both she and a police-man had failed to open the door, she was driven to try des-perate methods, and said, "Go and get mummy's keys," to Sheba. To the amazement of the watching crowd, the dog thrust her nose into Ann's handbag, picked up the keys and passed them out through the one-and-a-half inch gap at the top of the window.

CARL MILES' CAT, Blackie, made history by being the first cat to be given a government licence to talk. Carl first sus-pected Blackie had the talent when he was a kitten and spent months playing him recordings to encourage him to talk, eventually being rewarded when Blackie apparently said, "I love you." He would walk through the streets of Atlanta, Georgia, with the cat on his shoulder, and people would pay to hear him talk, but Miles fell foul of the police and had to go to City Hall to get a performance licence to contin-ue.

In Turkey, Kamile Mutluturk's cat Pala learned to speak for itself, surprising his mistress when he was five years old by leaping up on her and saying, "Mother, mother, moth-er," (in Turkish of course). Since then he has mastered his mistress's first name, that of her daughter, and the word 'father'. In India a circus owner claims to own a cat which has walked on its hind legs since birth.

IN WASHINGTON STATE, USA, Greg and Stephanie McKay got the shock of their lives when their campsite was attacked by a bear-like creature, eight feet tall, ugly and smelly with curly hair. In an interview after the assault Stephanie said, "You may think this sounds crazy, but the bear talked to us." It spoke in a high pitched voice that did not sound human and asked if they had permission to use the campsite. Even though they said they did, it told them to get off the property immediately, then stood on its back legs and hurled stones at them. "We ran like hell," Stephanie said.

FREDERICO THE GOAT came to a sticky end when he stood for mayor in the town of Pilar, 500 miles north-east of Brasilia. Standing as a protest candidate launched on the campaign trail by his owner, Petrucio Maia, he was leading the polls by a wide margin when he dropped dead in suspicious circumstances. Maia suspected he had been poisoned by rivals – especially since when Frederico had been driven through the town in a 50-car convoy, they'd shot at him.

PIGEONS in London seem to have discovered the advantages of the Underground system – they have regularly been seen travelling from stop to stop in tube trains. David Lawrence says that he has often seen pigeons hopping on to eastbound Circle Line trains, getting off at Baker Street to peck round for half an hour before crossing the platform and taking a train back, while Lorna Read saw one hop on a Northern Line train at King's Cross to travel to Euston. In the classic work *The Street Life of the London Pigeon* Eric Sims records regularly seeing a reddish pigeon jump onto his train at Kilburn to travel to Finchley Road, where it would always alight to join three other pigeons on the platform. Others have been observed to commute daily from Hammersmith Station to Goldhawk Road, where there is evidently a better quality of platform snack, before returning on another train.

WHEN ROZ BROWN collapsed in a diabetic coma her West Highland terrier, Holly, revived her by fetching her a bag of jelly babies, tipping two onto the floor by her head, then nudging her to rouse her. The sweets revived Mrs Brown enough to get a final handful out of the bag before going in search of something more substantial.

Even more vital was the action of Jack Fyfe's sheepdog, Trixie. When Fyfe, 75, was paralysed by a stroke at his home in Sydney, Australia, Trixie kept him alive for nine days by soaking a towel in her drinking bowl and draping it over her owner's face so that he could suck it. She remained at the foot of the bed the whole time except when Mr Fyfe called, "Water." When her bowl was dry, Trixie took water from the toilet. Fyfe was eventually rescued when he failed to turn up for a family dinner, and by that time he'd lost four stones in weight.

CHAPTER ELEVEN

Sweet Revenge

Sometimes the oppressed get their own back —
in the animal kingdom just as among humans.

A RACCOON scored a posthumous victory in Canada
after it was shot by James Albert Maxwell, 32. Maxwell shot
the beast near a pole supporting power lines on his farm,
and its corpse toppled onto the cables, causing a short which
sent a massive power surge down a wire the farmer was
holding, and killing him instantly.

A COUNCIL CLERK in Swansea Valley was thwarted in
his attempts to introduce new by-laws for local dog owners.
The papers were eaten by his dog after they were dropped
through his letter box.

GUIDE DOG Lucky, so named because of his repeated escapes from close scrapes, seems to have had it in for his owners – he guided four of them to their deaths. "Lucky led his first owner in front of a bus and his second off the end of a pier," said Ernst Gerber, who was retraining the Alsatian in Wuppertal, Germany. "He actually pushed his third owner off a railway platform just as the Cologne to Frankfurt express was approaching, and he walked his fourth owner into heavy traffic, before abandoning him and running away to safety." But Gerber explained, "Basically, Lucky is a damn good guide dog. He just needs to brush up on some elementary skills. Apart from the epileptic fits, he has a lovely temperament." Gerber was planning to match Lucky with a fifth blind owner when retraining was finished, but was not planning to tell them about the dog's past. "It would make them nervous, and that would make Lucky nervous," he said.

A RABBIT called Barney, weighing six pounds, subjected a nine-stone Rottweiler named Amy to a reign of terror in the garden of their home in Benfleet, Essex. Owner Sharon Beckett saw him in action. "He bit the dog so hard it drew blood, but Amy just ran away cowering and whimpering," she said. Barney kept up the rampage for a week before being confined to quarters. A vet diagnosed a frustrated mating urge.

"WE NORMALLY lock them in the bathroom to stop them wrecking the place while we're out," said despairing Stockholm resident Roger Sjoberg, after he came home to find that his two cats had indeed wrecked the place while he was out – despite having been locked in the bathroom. He found the house flooded and two frightened cats sitting on the shower taps, jamming them on, causing more than $60,000 worth of damage.

CATS IN ORANGE County, California, struck back at another ancient adversary. In a rare example of feline co-operation, a huge pack of wild cats ganged up and attacked a sleeping dog in Dana Point Boat Yard. Annie, a pit-bull/Labrador cross howled in pain as cats swarmed all over her, biting and scratching, until she was rescued by her owner.

IN VOLOGDA, Russia, a street thief got a major surprise when he tried to grab what looked like an attractive fur hat from the head of a passer-by. The victim's fur collar suddenly came to life and sank its claws and teeth into the hand of the thief, who turned tail and ran. The wrap turned out to be a Siamese cat whose owner had decided to take it on his walk as extra thermal protection against the sub-zero temperatures.

IF IT'S NOT CATS, it's mice. In Mantua, Italy, a family of mice got their own back on Renate Pancea, 66, by building their nest in his chimney, completely blocking it. Pancea was killed by the carbon monoxide fumes which built up in his house as a result – as were three of his relatives who were waiting in the house for a priest to come and give him last rites.

ANY RODENT would have to go a long way to beat the achievement of a woodchuck in Laconia, New Hampshire. Apparently the police received a report of "a suspicious-acting woodchuck that would not let people out of the building" at the municipal sewage works. An officer was sent to deal with the siege and on arriving apparently "determined that the animal needed to be euthanised and tried to run it over with his cruiser." This did not work. According to an employee at the plant, "When the officer got out after running it over, I think he thought it was dead. Then the thing sprung up and attacked him." The officer tried to escape by jumping up on the cruiser, but slipped, injuring his knee. He finally resorted to pulling his 9mm pistol and pumping the rebellious woodchuck full of lead, bringing a prompt end to its brief reign of terror.

THE DARWIN MUSEUM in Australia, was the scene for an appropriately Darwinian struggle. Among the animals in the zoo's displays was Goddess, a Western Taipan, one of the deadliest snakes known to man, who was regularly fed live mice as part of her diet. One mouse, however, decided to get one in first, and on finding itself dumped into Goddess's tank it promptly sank its teeth into the snake's head. Although not fatal, these wounds then became infected, causing Goddess's face to balloon to vast proportions. The serpent had to fight for her life while the museum's curator carried out a series of six operations in an attempt to save her. The mouse did not live to see its triumph: Goddess had scoffed it a long time before she succumbed to the infection.

SNAKES also get their chance for revenge. In Harare, Zimbabwe, a cobra amazed animal experts by swallowing a mongoose. A baffled expert said, "A mongoose usually makes mincemeat of snakes."

In Warakapola, Ceylon, another snake extracted a much subtler form of revenge on its tormentor. A local house owner tried to deal with a cobra lurking outside his front door by beating it with a stick, but he failed to kill it and the venomous creature slithered off into the jungle. According to Ceylonese folklore cobras always seek revenge, and it certainly seemed to hold true in this case for within days four of the snakes had taken up permanent station around the house. The family were forced to employ a snake charmer to get rid of the cobras, but he only managed to capture two. No sooner had he left than, once again, four cobras appeared and took up their positions around the house, just sitting there... waiting.

IN KERALA, Southern India, snakes have also made a special target of Kizhakkumkara Veettil Omana, a widow who works in a cashew factory. She was bitten for the first time at the age of fourteen, and has been bitten twenty times since, usually by cobras but twice by vipers. Tiring of this repeated ordeal she consulted an astrologer, who told her that she was under the snake god's curse due to misdeeds committed by her ancestors and warned her that the 21st bite would be fatal.

Up to that point she had forbidden her sons from killing any snakes, even those which had bitten her, but now they say the next snake to come close to her will die. Omana and her family await their venomous visitors with clubs and big sticks. Each night they inspect every inch of their ramshackle hut for cracks and they clear the vegetation around the house every week to prevent any snakes hiding there. "I just have to strike first," says Omana. "I might not get another chance."

SHOWMAN Le Grand Melvin got more than he bargained for when he tangled with a snake. Melvin, whose real name was Jean Guy Leclair, used an eight-foot boa constrictor as a part of his stage act, during which he would be dressed up as a vampire and performed what were described as "morbid acts". One night in front of an audience of 150 people the snake got the upper hand when Melvin's routine went awry.

"He seemed to miss a reflex and the boa wrapped around his neck," said Gaetan Grenon, the manager of the cabaret. He noticed that Leclair was turning blue and called the police, who arrived within minutes. As four officers struggled to free the suffocating entertainer, Grenon cut off the snake's head with a knife, but unfortunately Leclair was already dead and could not be revived. The room in which Leclair performed "emptied out" as soon as the audience realised that he had lost control of the snake, Mr Grenon said. "There wasn't much panic really, they were just sort of shocked."

A FERRET being used for medical research in Chicago got its own back on the doctor who injected it with a respiratory virus. As the doctor was bending over it to look for signs of infection the ferret sneezed in his face, giving him the virus too.

WHEN DUDLEY HANDLEY arrived to open up his sporting goods store, which sold all manner of hunting paraphernalia, he found that a deer had got there first. It had crashed in through a window and was devastating the place. With the help of police he managed to corner it in a side room. When released, the buck left the shop through the window by which it had entered – the one advertising deer hunting licences.

In Dreux, France, another deer took an even more direct route to revenge. As Jean-Marie Macron followed beaters flushing out deer for him and his companions, he was unprepared for the speed at which one buck rocketed out of the brush. The buck, weighing more than 400 pounds, charged Mr Macron and gored him with his antlers before he was able to get off a shot. The wound severed the hunter's aorta and he bled to death within minutes. And in Trento, Italy, poacher Marino Malerba shot a stag as it stood above him on overhanging rocks. It fell off, landed on top of him and broke his neck.

SAMMY the shark also met his end from an unlikely quarter: he was eaten by a goldfish. The miniature shark was bought, along with a shoal of tropical fish, by Staffordshire publican Jim Bishop as a present for his wife, Linda. The new arrivals were put into a tank which already contained five goldfish. Within hours the five fish had scoffed all the new tropicals, and when Linda looked for Sammy he was missing too. "All you could see was his tail sticking out of a goldfish's mouth," she said.

IN IRAN a scorpion managed to poison an entire family in one go, sending all five to hospital in a serious condition. Hadi Zade, the mother of the family, was making a pot of tea, beginning by rinsing the pot in hot water, but she failed to notice that there was a scorpion lodged securely in the spout. When she made the tea the boiling water hit the scorpion, causing it to release its toxins into the tea in shock, so that when the family drank the brew they were all poisoned.

AN ELEPHANT in Karlsruhe Zoo reached through the bars of his cage with his trunk and turned on the hot water tap in the neighbouring hippo enclosure. As the hippo pool filled with scalding water, 28-year-old Purzel repeatedly hurled his two ton bulk against the pen, but it was Sunday night and no one was there to hear. By morning, Purzel, his mate and their one-year-old baby had boiled to death.

Pissed Again

Drink and drugs may seem to be exclusively
human passion — but just a glimpse at our
files reveals half the animal kingdom getting
out of its tree too.

BILLY THE GOAT got more than he bargained for when
he tucked into a feast of elderberries which were hanging
over a wall close to where he was tethered. He scoffed the
lot, but the feast fermented in his stomach and Billy keeled
over, hopelessly drunk. His owners, Dennis Hennigan and
Roy Dempsey of Bradley, Huddersfield, shortened his rope
so the berries were out of reach.

A 'BIG BLACK GOAT' in the town of Jotana in northern
Gujarat is a hardened smoker, and is in the habit of stealing

cigarettes from people to feed his addiction. "The sight," says reporter U. Mahurkar, "is bizarre. The goat puffs and inhales like any regular smoker." The beast apparently smokes 20 a day, given to him by local people, although he is not above snatching them for himself from unsuspecting victims, a habit which can be fairly disturbing if you are not expecting it. "Last fortnight, for instance, it scared the living daylights out of a camel-cart driver passing through the town when it leapt upon the moving cart from behind. The driver thought he was being attacked by a panther or some other wild animal until he saw it was actually a goat that was making a beeline for his ciggy."

AMELIA ROYBAL, of Albuquerque, New Mexico received a surprise when she went to answer the doorbell. She opened the door to a two-foot tall, very drunk monkey, who swaggered in and headed straight for the drinks cabinet. He poured himself a very large whiskey and downed it in one before heading back for more. "I thought it was a gag and someone was giving him signals," said the amazed Mrs Roybal, but the monkey, named Myron, continued drinking and became ever more aggressive. "He went bananas and my husband couldn't take the bottle from him," she said. They cornered him in the laundry room, but Myron retaliated by filling the washing machine with soap powder and flooding the room with suds. The Roybals called the law. When Deputy Sheriff Frank Garcia arrived, Myron was scoffing plastic fruit in the living room. As soon he saw a police uniform, he holed up in the pantry and started hurling potatoes and oranges at everyone with pin-point accuracy, holding his would-be capturers at bay until reinforcements arrived in the form of four more deputies. In the end, five deputies and seven Roybals were laying siege to the alcoholic primate and he was finally netted and taken to an animal shelter. There he remained huddled in a corner of his cage, clutching his head and groaning, staying like that or several days while his owner was sought. Amazingly, in this case he did turn out to be an escapee from one of those convenient and often mythical travelling circuses, and had got his taste for the hard stuff from his trainer who gave him a swig every nigh before he performed. "It's just to quieten his nerves before he faces an audience," he explained.

STAFF at Shaldon Zoo, Devon, were puzzled as to why their two cockatoos, Bobby and Cocky, always seemed to be reeling drunkenly, until they discovered that the birds' nesting boxes were made from old whisky barrels which were still giving off potent fumes. In Portsmouth it was another member of the parrot family, an African grey, that was getting out of its head, this time on dope. Police investigating the theft of the parrot from pensioner Judie Graham found cannabis plants sprouting in the aviary, growing from seed that she had fed the parrot. "Now I think of it, she did have some strong mood changes," said Judie.

DRUGS had a more serious effect on at least one bear in the Blue Ridge Mountains: it died after eating part of a cocaine shipment dropped into a Georgia forest by drug smugglers. The drugs were in a duffel bag which was part of a load dropped from a plane by a smuggler who died when his parachute failed to open as he bailed out. Gary Garner of the Georgia Bureau of Investigation said, "The bear got to it before we could and he tore the duffel bag open, got him some cocaine and OD'd. The bears have apparently scattered them (the packages) all over the hillsides. We don't know how many bears are involved. We know there was one because we found him. There's nothing left but big bones and a hide." Investigators said the black bear, weighing more than 50 pounds, had been dead about four weeks.

BEARS are pretty fond of booze too. In Nova Scotia a boozing bear systematically ransacked camps in remote Guysborough County. Five camps at least were broken into and at one camp, according to biologist Bob Bancroft, "The bear bit off the neck of a 40-ouncer, downed the contents and placed the empty back on the table – presumably hoping for a refill." The bear also dug up liquor caches buried around camps and drank them. To solve the problem, Bancroft suggested a leg-hold trap baited with a case of inexpensive wine, explaining: "Once a bear begins living off society, he must be snared or live-trapped and destroyed." In the Rocky Mountains, another biologist researching alcoholic bears left out cups of gin and bourbon as bait and watched amazed as a bear nonchalantly downed each in turn.

SMALLER woodland wildlife can also get a taste for booze, as demonstrated by the case of Scrumpy the Squirrel. Nursed back to health by Steve Wroot and his wife Deborah, who found it injured as a baby, the squirrel had the run of the house – and soon learned to prise the tops off cider bottles and drink the contents. Everything went fine until Steve decided to return the squirrel to the wild. As he tried to put the animal in a bag, fuelled by Dutch courage it went berserk and laid into him, biting and scratching. The frenzied creature beat Wroot off for two hours and cornered him in a bedroom. He had to jump 20 feet out of the maisonette window to get help from friends, but they too were driven back. Finally a woman from the

RSPCA bagged the crazed rodent in a sack. A society spokesman later said, "We are rehabilitating him from cider onto water and nuts. He will be released eventually."

ANOTHER RODENT with a drinking habit was a rat which hung out in the bar cellar of the Turk's Head on St Agnes in the Scilly isles. The rat chewed through the plastic pipe carrying the supply of stout up to the bar, and almost 80 pints of the stuff vanished overnight. Barman Tristan Hicks said, "I don't know how much he drank, but I couldn't find any puddles of booze left."

PERCY THE PIG was another cider casualty, developing a taste for the stuff after some was spilt on the carpet, and he went on to consume up to four cans a week. His indulgence got him evicted from his home in Clevedon near Bristol, after he repeatedly escaped from the garden of his owner, Aileen Osterholm, 32, and went rampaging through neighbouring gardens, trampling flowerbeds, vegetable patches and even chewing a canvas car cover, causing complaints to the council. Ms Osterholm said, "He escaped a couple of times when he was drunk.... We usually managed to get him back by rattling a can of cider. I don't think he caused any real damage – the neighbours were more worried about the smell." Percy was moved to a new home in Devon.

IN COMMUNIST ROMANIA an alcoholic cart-horse also caused vast problems for his owner after it became used to drinking low-quality beer by the bucketful during a surplus. The drunk horse neighed constantly, kicked, bit and generally became a menace to society. At first his owner, a carter, tied the horse to a tree outside his block of flats, but after it took to terrorising neighbours he moved it into the hall of the building, where it terrorised the inhabitants still more. Finally he moved it into his own flat – only to discover that it is impossible to cohabit with a drunken horse. Neighbours eventually got a writ to have the horse evicted and it was dragged out of the block, fighting all the way.

DONKEYS, too, can become addicted to the demon drink. In Sidmouth, Devon, a special sanctuary has been set up to treat donkeys for alcoholism. Owner Elisabeth Svendsen has treated animals used to a diet of Guinness and gin. "They get very aggressive and lose their normal placid temperament," she said. Among the animals she has treated are a group of three that came from a pub which had closed down. One of them was able to pick up a half-pint glass with its lips and drink its contents in one gulp.

WELLARD the beer-drinking cockerel was a regular at the Pointers, Newchurch, Isle of Wight, where he would down best bitter topped with crisps, then stagger happily round the pub. His antics caused considerable embarrassment on at least one occasion, when he mistook a customer's handbag for a hen and raped it. Landlady Pam White said, "There was no stopping him." When she gave up the pub soon afterwards Mrs White attempted to wean the boozy bird off drink, but the shock was too much and he dropped dead.

THE CHAMPION drunken farm animal has to be the cow. Brewster the bullock suffered a four-day hangover after overindulging in apples in the field where he lives. He ate so many that they fermented in his stomach, and his owner Maureen Russell found him lying unconscious on his back wearing a "happy leer". Mrs Russell said, "We just hope he doesn't suffer any liver damage." In Gloucestershire 18 cows were found staggering around with glazed eyes after eating sugar beet which fermented in their stomachs, and in Zimbabwe drunken cattle ran amok after drinking 100 litres of beer spilled when a brewery lorry ran off the road and hit an electricity pylon. Crazed cows chased a number of passers-by, but no one was hurt. In Northampton a bull which escaped from the town's cattle market fled into the Carlsberg brewery opposite and caused chaos, while a similar problem occurred in the Theakston's brewery at Masham, North Yorkshire. A bull brought in for a photo-shoot to advertise their new Black Bull beer went berserk and had to be shot. Finally, in Lajas, Puerto Rico, another herd of staggering cows worried a farmer until he discovered that they had stumbled upon a bale of marijuana dropped from a plane and had eaten it, mistaking it for hay.

AN ATTEMPT to smuggle cannabis into Zimbabwe went seriously pear-shaped when a long-distance lorry driver fell foul of a troop of baboons. Attracted by the smell of the drug, they stormed the truck where it was stashed and tore the tarpaulin off while it was stopped at a Zambian border post. The driver was jailed for six months. Another drug-smuggling mission went awry in Columbia. Carrier pigeons were being used to fly marijuana over the walls of a prison in the town of Buga, but the scheme was uncovered when one pigeon, overburdened with packets of dope, smacked into a wall.

THE LARGEST animal drinkers have to be elephants, which have a particular fondness for booze and will go to almost any length to get it. In Jhitka, an Indian elephant on a binge caused widespread damage as it sought more hooch to satisfy its urges. It had drunk gallons of home-brew and was out for more, going wild and smashing down huts in the village when it couldn't find it. One villager said, "I heard a loud roar and saw this huge trunk push through my door. It missed me by inches as he trampled through my hut, knocking it down. He then tore down every hut in the village – more than 30 in all." Several villagers were injured, but no one was killed and the plastered pachyderm ended up prancing in circles before passing out with a crash. Police were unable to do anything about the creature until it groggily awoke, subdued by a massive hangover, and was easily driven back into the forest.

ELSEWHERE IN INDIA people have not been so lucky. Booze-fuelled rampages by herds of elephants have killed many people. One herd intoxicated by fumes from an illicit still went wild in Bengal in 1995, trampling a bootlegger to death; while in Simbulbari, near Calcutta, five elephants killed a man as they tried to reach warm vats of newly brewed beer. They were driven off by villagers with drums and torches, but not before flattening eight huts.

IN THAILAND the elephants are not so interested in booze, but many of them are amphetamine addicts. Elephant handlers lace their charges' food with the stimulants so that they work faster and for longer hours in the logging industry. A special centre has been set up to rehabilitate the drug-addicted animals. An official there said: "Many of them go crazy when they need the drug."

Goodbye Cruel World

There are all sorts of records of animal suicides — as well as miraculous returns from the grave.

'HIGH-RISE CAT SYNDROME' claimed the lives of hundreds of New York cats and dogs during the 1994 heatwave. High temperatures and unbearable humidity caused the animals to hurl themselves off high buildings in a vain attempt to cool off. Not all the animal deaths that summer were heat-related, though. One hapless Pomeranian expired due to his owner cleaning his gun with nitro-glycerine (is that ever a good idea?) — he caused an explosion which catapulted the dog to its death out of a fifth-floor window.

IN ETHIOPIA hang-gliders are now banned from national parks — the antelopes mistake them for giant vultures and leap to their deaths in panic.

THOUSANDS OF FROGS in north-east Thailand killed themselves by leaping onto the spines of thorny bushes, causing considerable distress among villagers in the region, who regarded the occurrence as an evil omen. A similar mass-suicide in the same part of the country two years previously was followed by serious hardship in the region. Just before this event another herpetological holocaust caused despair in the south of the country. Ten thousand toads fought a massive battle, leaving huge numbers dead, an event which had last occurred just before the Japanese invasion of 1941.

IN CALIFORNIA it was turkeys who decided to off themselves *en masse*, rather than wait for the chop at Christmas. 13,000 of the 40lb birds were trampled to death as they crashed into barn doors and fences in a mad stampede. The ranch owner blamed a low-flying aircraft for panicking the creatures.

ITALIAN SHEEP also decided to become the masters of their fate rather than wait to become pre-packed portions. 200 of them jumped one by one into a fast-flowing river near Reggio Emilia, much to the bafflement of shepherds.

CHINESE SHEPHERDS in Mongolia really had their task cut out for them when their herd of sheep took it into their heads to commit mass suicide in a lake. Two goats with an apparent death-wish took the lead, jumping into the 5ft (1.5m) deep water, prompting the sheep to follow. Twenty herdsmen took part in a three-hour rescue which succeeded in saving 281 sheep, while another 249 animals, including 206 goats, drowned. Some of the rescued animals had to be restrained from jumping back into the water.

SQUIRRELS in New York State went into lemming mode in 1995, with hundreds of them getting squashed by motorists as they crossed busy roads in the Catskill Mountains. Road-cleaning crews took to counting each night's kill. On one night they found 156 squirrels on a three-mile stretch near Kingston, with another 280 getting totalled the following night; while on the main interstate highway a further 922 were flattened. Biologists were puzzled, with some suspecting that a month-long drought was forcing the creatures away from the dry valleys in search of water, while others thought they were simply at a peak of their 30-year population cycle and were fanning out to find new pastures.

OTHER RODENTS have been going in for mass offings as well. In the Golan Heights, Israel, mice were seen committing suicide in their hundreds in 1985. Scientists estimated that there must have been at least 250 million mice in the region and they were regularly observed leaping off cliffs and into fast-flowing streams in huge numbers. The scientists concluded this was their way of instinctively dealing with overpopulation.

RESCUERS battled for three hours to save a pregnant ewe stranded 150ft (45m) down a cliff on the Isle of Skye, with police, coastguards and mountain experts joining in. They safely heaved the animal to the top and were congratulated by grateful crofter Neilie McLure. When he turned to check on his animal, it dived back over the cliff to its death.

RATHER LARGER leapers are the walruses of Togiak Wildlife Refuge at Cape Pierce in Alaska. Every summer since 1994 they have been committing suicide over a 100ft

(30m) cliff. Forty-two went over the edge in 1994, another 17 in 95 and in 1996 225 tried to make their way up to the cliff, but wardens could only turn back 155 — the rest made it to their doom. They were part of a herd of 12,500 non-mating walruses which gather every summer to eat and sun themselves. As usual, biologists were baffled.

DOGS are also renowned as suicidal leapers of a particularly loyal kind. When 59-year-old Jean Ricord died of a heart-attack, his dog, a 17-year-old mongrel named Zouzou, was inconsolable. He sat whining on the balcony of their flat near Nice for days, then, as the funeral procession left the house, the dog jumped to his death. In Moscow a collie, distraught over its owner's death, threw itself out of a ninth-floor window and died.

FRITZ THE DACHSHUND went everywhere with his owner Amadeo Domancich, even when he tried to kill himself. Amadeo hurled himself from a fifth-floor window, closely followed by the ever-faithful Fritz, but while Amadeo survived with just a broken leg, Fritz was killed. "I'm even more depressed now," said the bereft Domancich.

WHILE SOME CREATURES are busy killing themselves, others are just as busy giving the Grim Reaper a hard time. Evelyn Thomas of Reading, Berkshire, recalled a childhood incident when her family went to Southend and bought some flounders home for supper. The fish were duly beheaded and floured ready for the frying pan, and the family were sitting in an adjoining room when they heard a weird noise from the kitchen. On investigating they found one of the prepared fish had flapped off the table and across the floor, and was bashing against the flour bin.

SAMMY THE GOLDFISH also made it back from the grave after his owner Fergal Parkinson, 19, found him floating on top of his bowl, stiff as a board. He placed the fish in an envelope and buried it under two inches of soil in his garden in Crookes, Sheffield. Forty minutes later Fergal noticed some movement beneath the soil and then Sammy's head appeared, followed by his wriggling body. The fish was quickly put back in his bowl where, after spitting out some earth, he began swimming vigorously again. Vets are puzzled by this piscine resurrection. In Goldsithney, near Penzance, six-year-old Sophie Nowall found a 'dead' goldfish lying in the gutter and took it home for a proper burial. As she rinsed the grit off the corpse it began wriggling and gasping for breath, so she popped it in water, where it thrived.

MORE THAN EIGHT MONTHS after the California earthquake of 17 January 1994 a charcoal-coloured white-dotted domino damselfish was discovered alive in a Santa Monica apartment. He had survived in an evaporating supply of dank water amid the decomposing remains of a handful of other fish and a hermit crab in a 60-gallon aquarium. Robert Madok and his sister Theresa had been barred from the Sea Castle apartment building because of severe quake damage, and when they were finally allowed in they discovered the fish in the gravel as they emptied the aquarium. They transferred him to a new tank and a week later he had grown from the size of a dime to that of a quarter.

NOT SO LUCKY was three-year-old Benjamin Ward's goldfish. The fish's bowl focused the morning sun's rays onto a set of dining-room curtains in the Wards' Doncaster home, igniting them and starting a fire which badly damaged the house. A fire officer said, "The thick glass must have acted like a magnifying glass. It's a very unusual case, but there is no other explanation." The fish did not survive.

IN PLEASANTON, California, the Lawson family took their cat Katrina to an animal shelter because their children had developed allergies to her. At the shelter the cat was put down by lethal injection and the corpse placed in the refrigerator to await collection by a rendering company. Five days later, Katrina casually strolled into the Lawson house, showing absolutely no ill effects. She had walked two miles from the shelter and had crossed a major freeway. "There simply is no explanation," said Richard Elliot, the shelter officer who had administered the injection to the cat. The Lawsons took the hint and kept Katrina, allergies or not.

FARMER Adrian Fry of Hutton Cranswick, Yorkshire, had seven cows die of heart attacks in one year, and suspected electric shocks were responsible. Cows have less resistance to electrical current than humans and suffer the effects long before we can feel them. Once he had two cows collapse, "shaking like jellies", as they were being milked. Despite his suspicions Yorkshire Electricity could find nothing. On Maple View Farm, in Avon, Maine, thirteen Holstein cows were killed rather more dramatically when a pole-mounted transformer burned out, sending a surge of power through a breeding barn. Meanwhile, a Mrs Culpepper of north London was causing considerable incredulity among her friends with a frozen food sighting – she claimed to have once come across a cow stone dead, frozen stiff and still standing up, but no one would believe her. She wrote to the papers appealing for corroboration.

JEFFREY JEROME was loved and cosseted all his life, but the 1100-pound pig suffered a death as predestined as any in a Greek tragedy. In 1988 Jeffrey was subject to a city ordnance which banned the keeping of pigs in Houston, Texas, and owner Victoria Herberta was forced to give him up for adoption, finding a comfortable home for him on a farm in San Marcos, 200 miles south. Jeffrey's real hang-up was lightning. "He was so afraid of storms," said Ada Davis, who owns the farm. He would tremble and hide at the onset of every storm, as if he knew one was fated to get him – and sure enough, one did. Jeffrey was barbecued by a bolt of lightning on 30 May 1994. "This is terrible," said Ada. "You could tell he'd been struck by lightning – he was kind of fried."

ARNOLD, a young pig from London, Kentucky, was far luckier. The pig, which belonged to Elizabeth Strunk, eight, had frozen to death in the garage a couple of days after she got him and was clinically dead when he arrived at the surgery of vet Campbell Mercer: his skin was purple, he wasn't breathing and he had no pupil response. There seemed to be nothing the vet could do so the Strunks took Arnold home for burial. When he got home from work, Elizabeth's father suggested soaking the animal in hot water as a last resort. Elisabeth soaked and massaged Arnold, and a few hours later he was squealing up a storm.

ALSO DEFROSTED in the nick of time was Valerie the chicken. Farmer Janet Bonney thought the chicken was dead when she found her frozen beneath her porch "Legs up, just as though you had got her from the freezer," she said. Mrs Bonney tried to put the chicken in a shoebox for burial, but the stiff legs wouldn't bend to let the lid fit, so she used a hot-water bottle to thaw the bird enough to bend. Then she felt a thump and heard a breath coming from Valerie. She gave the chicken mouth-to-beak resuscitation and three or four thumps on the chest, then warmed the bird further so that after three hours she was back on her feet and clucking again.

AN OKAPI named Katanda started hyperventilating, then collapsed and died in Copenhagen Zoo when performers from the Royal Theatre began rehearsing selections from Wagner's *Tannenhauser* in a park 300 yards away. The corpse was sent to Copenhagen University for stuffing, but was stolen and barbecued by students.

Too Much Monkey Business

The activities of our primate brethren are inventive and strange enough to warrant a chapter to themselves.

GANGS of wild monkeys have been causing havoc on farms outside Tokyo by regularly raiding them for apples. An agriculture department spokesman said, "They picked up the habit of feeding on apples after one raided an orchard last year – some have been seen carrying apples away in plastic shopping bags." Also near Tokyo a pack of monkeys, apparently desperate for food, raided a village and made off with mens' and womens' underwear from a washing line.

A CRATE of whisky and another of beer were missing from Vlooi Barnard's lorry when he arrived at a ranger post in South Africa's Kruger National Park with supplies, but he could not understand why. Nothing had fallen off and he had only stopped once on the way, to shoo some monkeys off the road. This was not the first time supplies had vanished either. On his next visit, when he again had to pull up for the monkeys, instead of yelling at them from his cab he jumped out. As he left the cab, he heard a rustle in the trees and turned to see two large apes drop onto his truck, grab a crate each and vanish into the bush — where he found local peoples waiting for them to hand over the swag. When arrested, they confessed to having trained the monkeys and apes to loot passing trucks.

SCIENTISTS at America's Harvard University have found out that rhesus monkeys can add and subtract, in an extended study involving aubergines.

WARDENS at Longleat safari park in Wiltshire had to show their male gorilla, Nico, blue movies of apes having sex in order to encourage him to mate with a female, Samba, as he was too shy to do it himself. No such encouragement was needed at Sandown Zoo on the Isle of Wight. There, management ordered zoo-keeper Sarah Wittington, 22, to cover up her top because they believed it was making one of the monkeys over-excited. She was luckier than 23-year-old Eva Amaya, who worked at Cordoba Zoo: she got fired when the male chimps started fighting for her attention.

OVER-EXCITED is probably too mild a word for the mood of one orangutan in Jakarta. He leapt onto and kissed a naked woman who was about to take a bath in a Borneo river. The woman, a widow named Mistin, screamed and fainted. She was rescued by villagers attracted by her cries, but she did not regain consciousness until she was back home in bed. It is clear, though, where apes' main interests lie. In Kuwait a servant girl was sexually assaulted by an ape who attacked her from behind as she did the laundry on the roof of her employer's house. She was unable to fight him off until a neighbour intervened and threw the beast a banana. "As soon as the ape got the banana his desire vanished," he explained.

AN ANONYMOUS French tourist was strolling with his wife in the orangutan sanctuary in Sandakan, Borneo, when Raja, a 14-year-old male orangutan, grabbed him and stripped him naked. The ape didn't disturb the man's wife. The Frenchman, in his 30s, kept still for fear of being attacked. Raja fled into the forest clutching trousers, shirt and underwear while the tourist rushed to the park office where someone lent him a pair of trousers. A park official said that Raja was not violent, but could be 'inquisitive' at times. It was the first time such an incident had occurred in the park, he said, but he advised visitors not to wear clothes which could be easily removed.

ANOTHER ORANGUTAN tried the subtle approach. Dr Gary Shapiro, vice-president of the Los Angeles-based Orangutan Foundation International, developed a close relationship with Rinnie, a female orangutan, as he tried to teach her sign language in the Borneo jungle. "On my 27th birthday," said the psychologist, "she came up to me and actually greeted me as I swam across the river. She took me by the hand, walked me across a dry swamp and took me behind a tree. There, on the ground, she had constructed a day nest which was larger than normal. She lay down on the bed, spread her legs and started pulling me towards her. It was a definite proposition. I signed her 'No' and she looked at me with those big eyes. She knew that I had scorned her. From then on she was much colder, not nearly as affectionate, and just very businesslike, although she did get over it." Shapiro described Rinnie as "nice-looking and good-natured as orangutans go." Fellow orangutan researcher Dr Birtute Galdikas was said to have joked on Shapiro's return to camp: "Gary, you should have done it for science."

TRANS-SPECIES LUST had a grimmer climax for Romeo, a monkey which frequented the SMGS hospital in Jammu, north-west India, where he had developed a taste for biting and pinching the female patients, and groping nurses. Because monkeys are sacred to Hindus, he was allowed to swagger around the hospital unmolested, but eventually after more than sixty assaults had taken place the staff's tolerance cracked, and they went on strike to demand action. Faced with the hospital's closure the authorities put out a shoot-to-kill contract on Romeo's head. It proved harder to carry out than expected. First followers of the Hindu monkey god Hanuman sabotaged the police's attempts to get a clear shot at the animal; then, sensing people were out to get him, Romeo sloped off and tried to blend in with a troupe of other monkeys. He would have succeeded, but his urges got the better of him and he sneaked back into town and assaulted another woman. Witnesses called the police who immediately gave chase, cornering Romeo on a window-sill after a 45-minute pursuit and killing him with a shotgun.

SOME SAY our railways are run by apes, but in South Africa this was literally true for a while. After railwayman

James Wide lost his legs in an accident on the track at Port Elizabeth, South Africa, in the 1870s, he became signalman at Uitenhage Tower and lived in a small shack beside the signal box. He was accompanied only by a huge baboon known as Jack, who assisted Wide in every way. The animal pumped water from the well, did the housework and dug the garden. Eventually Wide decided to see if he could get the ape to deal with the signal box too, showing him how to operate the signal levers and controls which opened and closed the switches on a siding. Jack became so good at the job that he ran the signal box for nine years without making a single serious mistake. More recently, the owner of a petrol station in Ibidan, Nigeria, had a chimp which was trained to fill cars with petrol and take the money.

IT'S NOT JUST manual work that apes excel at. In Sweden a newspaper gave five stock analysts and a chimpanzee the equivalent of $1250 each to make as much money as they could on the stock market. After one month the chimp, named Ola, saw the value of his stocks rise by $180, while his nearest rival, the publisher of the stock market magazine *Bourse Insight,* only made $130. While the stock experts pored over their portfolios, Ola made his brilliant decisions by hurling darts at a list of all the companies on the Stockholm stock exchange.

THE ART WORLD also has several apes competing with the old masters in the sale rooms. Charles, a 440lb gorilla living in the African pavilion of Toronto Zoo, paints pictures commanding up to £365 a canvas. Charles's keeper, Vanessa Phelan, said he had been painting since he was young, but his art didn't take off until he was introduced to the colour black in 1991. "He is a knuckle-worker," she said. "He uses the back of his knuckles to paint and an authentic Charles will have either a footprint or a handprint in it." Artworks by the orangutan Nonia from Vienna Zoo are even more valuable, fetching up to £900 each and gaining him a contract to design wine labels for a local vineyard.

THE APE WORLD is not without its delinquents either. In Liverpool, New South Wales, police chased a car with a grinning chimp sitting in the passenger seat until it crashed through a fence and into a house. The chimp fled up a tree and remained there until coaxed down by two police officers. The driver, who had a blood alcohol level way over the legal limit, did not own the chimp and could not explain how it came to be in his car. In New Orleans, Zippy the performing chimp gave his owners the slip and went for a night on the town wearing tennis shoes and blue underwear. Police called by Zippy's worried owners finally found him riding round the streets with four youths in a van. They had picked him up after finding him outside a grocery store, smoking a cigar.

A ROGUE monkey in the Himalayan town of Udhampur caused widespread mayhem, attacking people at random and seriously injuring 17 women and children. According to a hospital spokesman, the animal had "almost gouged out the eyes of a three-year-old and injured her mother's private parts." The fiend always struck around noon, after the menfolk had gone to work, and townspeople were afraid to leave their homes after the men had left.

JACKO the monkey evaded capture for over two weeks in Georgetown, Guyana, despite the efforts of angry residents. They were infuriated by his habit of breaking into houses, sampling cosmetics, messing up kitchens, trying on condoms and making vulgar gestures. He carried out at least 20 burglaries during his period of freedom.

IN SIMLA, India, a monkey grabbed a bag of money from a trader and scattered it from the rooftops. A crowd scrambled for the 100-rupee notes that rained down while the trader looked on helplessly. He had withdrawn the money from the bank and was going home when the monkey snatched the bag, presumably thinking it held food.

A SCHOOLTEACHER in the Calcutta suburb of Domjur shot a monkey that entered his garden, fatally wounding it. The animal crawled to an adjacent police compound and lay there writhing until local people took it to a veterinary clinic, where it died. When the corpse was brought back to the police station more than fifty monkeys gathered outside, shrieking loudly, and refused to leave for hours. A local Communist politician, apparently moved by the animals' protest, fled a formal complaint asking the police to arrest the teacher, but they took no action.

ACCORDING to the Ugandan *New Vision* newspaper, a man named Okecho killed a baboon which was damaging his maize and banana plantations, leaving the animal dead in his compound. More than thirty other baboons converged on the place and "mourned like human beings" before carrying their fallen comrade into the forest. Neighbours reported that the animals then returned and stormed the farmer's house, knocking down the door. A *New Vision* reporter who reached the scene claimed he saw Okecho lying in a pool of blood with a huge hole in his chest where the baboons had ripped his heart out.

THE SAUDI newspaper *Okaz* reported that a man driving to work in the Khamis Mesheit region ran over one of a troupe of monkeys roaming the southern desert. When the remaining monkeys spotted his car on the return journey, they jumped on it and smashed the windows with their fists. In Penang, too, monkeys were out for revenge. The day after a youth in a yellow shirt had stoned a young monkey to death, a group of sixty others attacked any joggers and visitors wearing yellow.

THE TABLES were turned at Seneca Park Zoo, Rochester, New York, when a 425-pound orangutan named Gambar made his bid for freedom. He ripped apart a sliding metal door on his cage and escaped, to romp around the zoo. As he did so fifty terrified spectators rushed into the ape house and shut themselves in until officials were able to subdue the exuberant ape with tranquilliser darts half an hour later.

INDIAN OFFICIALS preparing for parliamentary elections had their work halted by hordes of monkeys which destroyed office equipment and documents. Delhi's chief electoral officer T. T. Joseph said the marauders had ripped the curtains off polling booths and shoved officials about. "We are apprehensive that they will damage valuable election material such as electoral rolls, paper and stamps," he said. They hired a private security firm who looked into ways of removing the monkeys humanely. They intended to immobilise the monkeys with sprays, then drive them away with air guns.

Animal Crackers

There are some animal stories which simply
defy categorisation

TWO MALE STORKS in Osnabruck Zoo, Germany, built a nest – and used it to hatch an abandoned penguin egg.

A HORSE wedged in an alley in Rochdale, Lancashire, bolted to freedom when it was startled by a frog jumping on its back, while in Montmelon, Switzerland, farmer Karl Wegner was confused by his goats' behaviour – they were constantly leaping over the backs of cows tied up in his byre.

NEAR PORT ELIZABETH, South Africa, over 2000 people flocked to a remote village to see a 'talking goat', said to be a debt-ridden man transformed by a witch-doctor.

PALESTINIAN FARMER Mufeed Sheik had his financial problems solved after he was cut off from his construction job in Israel when the government sealed off the West Bank after a terrorist attack — his billy-goat developed a milk-producing udder. The goat, named Abu Mosa'id, was male in every respect and had sired fifty kids, but had one teat which produced two glasses of milk a day. When news of this got out the rumour spread that the milk could cure impotence, and Mufeed took to selling it for $50 a glass. He fed the animal on a special diet of fruit and vegetables, but slaughtered it when he could no longer stand the pressure of people descending on his village day and night.

FAINTING GOATS have undergone a major resurgence in the American Midwest in recent years. The beasts have been specially bred to keel over when surprised, undergoing a fainting fit lasting just fifteen seconds. Afterwards they get up and continue as if nothing has happened. The breed originated when flocks of sheep were under threat from wolves and coyotes. Farmers would put a fainting goat with the flock so that if they were attacked by predators the goat would faint and be eaten while the more valuable sheep fled. Today they are valued as pets and there is even a Fainting Goat Association in Iowa — to join you must send a photo of a comatose goat. Goat-fainting competitions are apparently being considered.

A DEPUTY HEADMASTER playing golf in Porthcawl caused himself and his opponent considerable surprise on the 17th hole — but not half as much as he caused a local sheep. When he teed off he drove the ball straight up the animal's bottom, causing it to bolt in terror. It ran thirty yards and deposited the ball on the green near the hole.

DINERS at the Avondale Riverside Hotel, Bathford, in Avon, got rather more than they bargained for when road-building disturbed an 18th-century graveyard in the grounds. The bodies were exhumed before work started but some bones were left behind, with predictable results. Hotelier Maddie Bell explained: "The dogs are always finding them and bringing them inside. It's really frightening and unpleasant for people." She was suing the Department of Transport after her customers were confronted by a dog clutching a human skull in its jaws.

WHEN DREAMER, his two-year-old Charolais heifer, went missing, farmer Vincent Balfe spent three weeks looking for her, eventually deciding he must have sold her by mistake at a local cattle market. Five months later, as the farmer's hay shed was being cleared, Dreamer emerged from among the bales. She was thought to have wandered into the shed as the hay was being stacked and become trapped. She had lost 450 pounds, apparently surviving by eating hay and twine, but seemed to have managed without any liquids at all. Normally a cow wouldn't last more than three weeks without water. Local vet Tommy Murphy said, "It was as if she had hibernated. She could stand and, while thin, was not emaciated." She soon put on a hundred pounds and appeared none the worse for her experience.

FARMER JOHN COOMBS discovered that hair began to sprout again on his bald patch after it had been licked by his cows. Inspired by the news of this new growth, Guy Tolson, a farmer from Ghent in Belgium, smeared damp salt on his head to encourage his cows to lick it, and he too regrew a full head of hair.

NEARLY 500 pigs were blown up or burned to death in Granada, Spain, when an electrical short circuit ignited methane gas produced by their dung.

PARIS ELECTRICIAN Etienne Warry spent six months teaching his parrot Emile to say "Long Live Liberty!" Immediately afterwards, though, Emile escaped and perched in a thirty-metre pine tree outside Warry's house, squawking "Long Live Liberty!"

KENYAN ARTIST and conservationist Mike Bukara has a new use for elephant dung: making paper. He boils it, crushes it until it reaches a porridge-like consistency, then rolls it out and sun-dries it. He uses the coarse brown paper for his wildlife paintings, and the Kenyan wildlife service sent out invitations to its 50th anniversary bash on the stuff. Even more amazing is the use Walsall pensioner Ivy Jones has for elephant dung – she keeps it in her bra to cure her arthritis. She asked Dudley Zoo for some after dreaming of the cure, and apparently it restored movement to her shoulder.

A THREE-LEGGED greyhound called Patch made his views known at the Maryhill warehouse belonging to Glasgow's Museum of Modern Art. The two-year-old stray slipped into the art store when the door was open and took exception to a work by Niki de Saint-Phale called 'Autel du Chat Mort' (Dead Cat's Altar). It was not the subject matter that drew Patch's disapproval, it was more the material used to create the artwork – particularly a stuffed grey cat. He seized the creature and made off with it. Despite his leg shortage, museum staff still had to chase Patch round the storehouse and 'half-way down Lochburn road' before they could grab the cat from his mouth.

RUSSIAN SCIENTISTS managed to breed amphibious chickens, according to a report in the newspaper *Tass*. "After a full training course," said Dr Igor Charkovski, who conducted the test, "the offspring not only swam and dived freely, but even ate and slept, and in a word lived under water. Everyone is amazed to see a chicken... ducking under and calmly pecking at grain thrown to the bottom of the pool. It seldom surfaces for air."

A PLAGUE of crows has been tormenting Moscow. They like to slide down the gold cupolas of the Kremlin churches and their claws are ruining the ancient gilt. Recordings of crows' warning cries have been played to frighten them away, but have had little effect. In Tokyo, over 20,000 jungle crows are causing havoc across the city. The birds rip open bin bags, steal laundry off clothes-lines, bomb pedestrians with their droppings, keep people awake by shrieking all night and even disrupt train services by placing pebbles on the line. The birds also get aggressive in the breeding season, swooping on pedestrians to drive them away from their nests, causing bruising and twisted ankles.

THIS ONE, it has to be said, sounds like an urban legend. A Hungarian couple bought a cuddly white 'puppy' at the Polish Market in Budapest – which will, it seems, sell you anything from Russian machine-guns to towels. Taking their new pet for its vaccinations, they told the vet that it had a huge appetite and was becoming vicious. He had to explain that this was not too surprising as the 'puppy' was in fact a polar bear cub. "It's just possible for this to happen," said Bruno van Puienbroeck, keeper of mammals at Antwerp Zoo. "There are a lot of polar bears on the market at the moment because many zoos want to get rid of them"

CHAPTER FIFTEEN

ZOE, an eight-month-old West Highland Terrier and a male despite the name, was found to emit sound from his ears, puzzling his owner, Raymond Burrows of Belfast, and the local vet Ian Millar, who had never heard of anything like it. Vets at the Animal Health Trust in Newmarket had, though. They had a five-year-old Welsh pony called Misty who was doing exactly the same thing. Tim Phillips described the sound as "a sort of screeching sound, like you get when there's feedback from an amplifier." The condition is known as 'whistling ear syndrome' and is a sort of reverse tinnitus. There is no known cure, but most of the time the affected animals don't seem to be bothered by it. The condition has also turned up in guinea-pigs and bats, and occasionally in humans – a couple in Leicestershire called an engineer to repair their TV set before discovering that the whining sound was coming from their child's ears.

TIRED of watching people flood to the nearby Royal Tyrell Museum of Dinosaurs, the 177 residents of Torrington, Alberta, opened the Gopher Hole Museum. It has 31 displays, featuring 54 stuffed gophers portraying scenes of every-day life in Torrington. They play hockey and baseball, get a hair-do, preach a sermon, fly-fish, shoot pool in a local tavern, rob a bank ("put your paws up") and lunch at a local cafe ("boy, are we stuffed").

References

THE BEASTS BITE BACK

Sheep attacks *D. Telegraph* 16 Feb 1994, *Times* 29 Jun 1996, *Independent* 20 Aug 1994. Bad moos *Weekend* 31 Feb 1979. Faint elk *S. Express* 26 mar 1995. Pit gopher *St Louis Post-Dispatch* 22 Jan 1985. Three-legged mouse *Laboratory News* 3 Sept 1982. Ferret Elect. *Telegraph* 3 May 1996. Violent seafood *Morning Sentinel* 3 July 1981, *D. Mirror* 28 Aug 1979, *S. Mirror* 8 Jan 1995. Cod almighty *D. Mirror* 23 Feb 1989, Shark dinner *Houston Chronicle* 24 Aug 1988. Boisterous barracuda *USA Today* 14 Jul 1993. Bombed *S. Mail* 21 Apr 1996, *D. Mail* 24 Feb 1996. Swoop *D. Telegraph* 14 Feb 1995, *Toronto Globe & Mail* 12 Aug 1993. Swan smash *S. Post* 9 May 1993. Messy proposal *S. Mail* 3 Nov 1996. Hell Toupee *W. Morn. News* 26 Aug 1992. Denture adventure *Dagbladet* 10 Feb 1992. Cock eared *Times of Oman* 16 Feb 1995. Explosions *Dundee Courier & Advertiser* 10 Jan 1985, *Eve. Post* 28 Aug 1985. Hell's hippo *Guardian* 27 Jan 1995. Phone croc *D. Mail* 15 Jun 1996. Zebra *[AFP]* 14 Oct 1996. Roo balls *D. Mirror* 1 Feb 1991.

TOUCH OF MYSTERY

Monkey puzzle *Source unknown* 21 July 1994. Deep Freeze mice *D. Mail* 15 Jul 1982. Blue swans *Sun* 3 Apr 1990. Ghost tree *Stocksbridge Trader* 13 Jul 1995. Sensible snails *Theosophical Review* 15 Jan 1903. Discerning goat *Titbits* 5 Jan 1980. Teleporting goat *Express & Star* 20 May 1980. Death omen *Richmond & Twickenham Times* 29 Oct 1976. Bee omen *D. Mirror* 11 May 1989. Spirit owl *World Herald* 21 Sept 1984. Shark salute *Independent* 31 Dec 1993. Pigeon crash *S. Wales Argus* 3Aug 1996. Stiff starlings *D. Post* 7 & 8 Dec 1992, Bird fall *[PA]* 22 Oct 1992. Hare ring *D. Telegraph* 14 Mar 1992. Cat ring *Letters, Fortean Times 51* Winter 1988/89. Cat escape *S. Express* 17 Jul 1977. Foxgloves *Reville* 20 Feb 1976.

DUMB ANIMALS

Dopey dobie *D. Mirror* 28 Sept 1988. Daft deer *Houston Chronicle* 22 Sept 1985. Moronic moose *Duluth (MN) News-Tribune* 6 Oct 1996. Persistent porcupine *S. Express* 15 Nov 1981. Risky rottweiler *NY D. News* 17 Nov 1994. Dumb dinners *Sun* 20 Sept 1995, *S. Express* 20

Aug 1995, *[AP]* 26 Jan 1994. Stone swallower *D. Telegraph* 27 Apr 1996. Car cruncher *S. People* 30 Dec 1984. Pen puffer *"Some New York Paper"* Mar 1995. Grotty guards *D. Telegraph* 10 Mar 1995, *S. Mail* 10 Sept 1995. Jammed moo *D. Star* 12 Sept 1994. Cowabunga! *D. Mail* 30 Sept 1995, *Zimbabwe Herald* 18 Nov 1994. Otterly stupid *D. Mail* 22 Mar 1988. Light lunch *San Francisco Chronicle* 15 Aug 1986. Crap carp *Today* 29 Jun 1995. Squirrel assault *FT 100* July 1997. Green greed *D. Telegraph* 11 Feb 1982.

THE GOAT IN THE MACHINE

Light Bears *Guardian* 19 Nov 1993. Plane moose *M'boro Eve. Gazette* 8 Feb 1997. Mike bat *D. Telegraph* 11 Sept 1996. Boat bugs *Today* 23 July 1997, Wild wallabies *D. Star* 12 Sept 1994, Sheep crash *Yorks. Post* 5 Apr 1995, Bike bear *D. Telegraph* 16 Jun 1981, Biker Dog *Mirror* 1 Feb 1986, Driving dogs *Toronto Globe* 31 Dec 1994, *S. Mail* 14 Apr 1994, *Today* 9 Aug 1994, *NY Post* 14 Sept 1993, *D. Express* 8 Apr 1988, *D. Telegraph* 24 Jun 1995, Digger pigs *Weekend Telegraph* 13 Apr 1996, *EDP* 14 Jun 1997. Electric chicken *Celeb* 28 Jul 1988. Piranha power *The Sun* 11 Apr 1980. Rodent rage *Halifax Eve. Courier* 12 Apr 1997. Horse power cut *Guardian* 19 May 1994. Giraffe phone *Weekend* 18-24 March 1981. Wired mutt *Internet message* 18 Dec 1993. 999 dog *[AP]* 13 Mar 1996, *D. Mirror* 22 Apr 1993, *NY Post* 15 Jan 1992. Worm Drive *Eastern Eve. News* 13 May 1996. Astro peckers *[AP]* 3 Jun 1995. Alarm birds *D. Telegraph* 16+22 May 1996. Ultraparrot *D. Mirror* 30 Sept 1991.

ON THE RAMPAGE

Highway robbery *Independent* 5 Jul 1991. Rail rage *[AP]* 22 Feb 1993. The Birds *Aberdeen Press & Journal* 26 Mar 1993. Et Dog *[AP]* 20 Jun 1993. Frog paddy *D. Telegraph* 6 Jun 1981. Off their trolley *S. Express* 11 Jun 1995. Bath Goat *The Australian* 13 Nov 1978. Killer pandas *Le Soir* 23 Aug 1995. Jack the Flipper *D. Telegraph* 10 Mar 1995, Sun 21 Apr 1995, *Today* 10 Dec 1994. Terrapin terror *D. Telegraph* 21 Apr 1997, *D. Record* 5 Aug 1995. Savage Squirrels *D. Star* 6 Mar 1995. Pig flap *FT74:11 No source.* Sheep craze *D. Mirror* 12 Sept 1977. Penguin panic *D. Mail* 25 Jun 1990, *Audubon mag.* Date unknown.

HOW DID THEY GET THERE?

Trouser mouse *Carlisle News & Star* 29 Nov 1994. Brassed-off gerbil *D. Mirror* 2 Feb 1995. Pipe bear *EDP* 7 Jul 1983. Toad spout *Surrey Hants News* 16 Sept 1980, *Newbury Weekly News* 25 Oct 1888. Funny Bunny *S. Mail* 29 Jan 1989, *D. Telegraph* 25 Aug 1978. Lazy Leopard *M'bro Eve Gaz* 8 Jan 1995, *USA Today* 14 Oct 1993. Ear wedged *[AP]* 28 Feb 1996, *Guardian* 24 May 1988. Ear spider *Bangkok Post* 9 Apr 1993. Flat mouse *D. Star* 29 Jan 1993. Flying pig? *The Register (Santa Anna, California)* 26 Feb 1982. Super sealion *San Francisco Chronicle* 22 Mar 1980 Stranded seals *New Scientist* 15 Jan 1994. Genoa penguins *D. Telegraph* 7 Jan 1995, *Wolverhampton Express & Star* 9 Dec 1994. Flying fish *Rand D. Mail* 16 Aug 1982, *Eve. Post* 20 Apr 1988. Wooly jumper *S. Express* 15 Jul 1990. Flying feline *Weekend Telegraph* 24 Sept 1994. Trapped cat *D. Telegraph* 30 May 1996. Caterwauling *D. Mail* 28 Oct 1995. Tree cat *Independent* 9 Sept 1996. Trouser snake *San Antonio Express News* date unknown, *Halifax Eve. Courier* 12 Apr 1995.

RESCUED

Pigs overboard *The Times (Ontario)* 21 Jan 1898. Crash pig *Unknown* Bitsy *D. Star* 18 Sept 1992. Ball dog *Independent* 8 Aug 1995. Dog fish *Leics. Mercury* 18 May 1995. Tree hound *D. Express* 16 Feb 1995. Dog doc *NY Daily News* 4 Dec 1989. Dog leg *Western Mail* 26 Jan 1995. Lion rescue *Weekend* 29 Jun-5 Jul 1977. House cat *Independent* 2 Aug 1995. Falls *Int. Herald Tribune* 20 Apr 1996, *S. Express* 20 Nov 1977. Raccoon bounce *Omana World Herald* 25 Oct 1990. Piss bomb *Las Provincias (Spain)* 14 Sept 1995. Chihuahua mum *[AP]* 18 Jul 1996, 26 Jun 1996. Rabbit fostering *W'hampton Express & Star* 9 Apr 1996. Defensive geese *S. Express* 21 Jul 1985. Ray rescue *Unknown*. Turtle *Today* 2 Mar 1991.

SWARM!

Hare *Army Weekend* 7-18 Feb 1968, Satanic snakes *People* 20 Nov 1994. Stung mourners *D. Mirror* 11 Sept 1995, *Boston S. Globe* 26 Jan 1997. Badger siege *D. Mail* 28 Dec 1995. Mozzie snuff *Lincoln (Nebr.) Star* 5 Aug 1988. Termites and terrorists *Times* 27 Sept 1996. Romanian raiders *Electronic Telegraph* 18 Mar 1997. Chimney dive *Anchorage D. News* 13 May 1993. Crabs *Cornish & Devon Post* 23 May 1987. Crawlin' crawdads *Portland (ME) Press-Herald* 13 May 1985. Crabs again *D. Telegraph* 4 Sept 1991 Dam mice *[R]* 8 Sept 1993. Mouse plague *D. Telegraph* 1980. No pied piper *D. Mirror* 13 Jun 1991. Termite terror *S. China Morning Post* 10 Nov 1994.

SEX BEAST
Fish Fuck *EEN* 6 Jan 1996, Ferry lust *The Record* 29 Oct 1989. Bulls rape car *Expressen* 31 May 1996. Bull bang *Scottish Sun* 18 Jun 1996, Seal shag *Europa Times* Apr 1994, Doomed *D. Record* 28 Jul 1995, *Weekly World News* 28 Jun 1988, *D. Mirror* 1 Apr 1985, *Europa Times* Jun 1994. Rhino rape *D. Star* 8 Jun 1994, *New Scientist* 20 Jul 1996. Octopoofs *New Scientist* 22 Oct 1994. Gay giraffes *Guardian* 14 Jun 1985, *D. Express* 13 Feb 1981. Sheep shagging *Guardian* 28 Nov 1994,. Pink sheep *S. Telegraph* 9 Mar 1997, *New Scientist* 10 Nov 1990. Undie sheep *D. Record* 9 April 1993. Stars *D. Mirror* 17 Sept 1994, *D. Star* 9 Jun 1994. Tortoise terror *Playboy (US)* April 1983. Frog frenzy *Philedelphia (PA) Daily News* 4 Sept 1996, *The Sun* 7 May 1996, *D. Telegraph* 16 Jul 1994. Bear Rape *[PA]* 4 Dec 1992. Rabid racoon rape *Glasgow Eve. Times* 6 Jun 1996. Odd dogs *[AP]* 3 Nov 1993. Hound orgy *D. Mirror* 21 Feb 1995.

ALMOST HUMAN
Hot Gulls *News of the World* 28 Aug 1980. Doc Ock *S. Times* 9 Jun 1996. Wash 'n' crow *D. Star* 21 Dec 1994. Sheep ram *S. Express* 6 Jun 1982. Bookhound *Newport News D. Press* 29 Nov 1993. Dog thieves *S. Mail (Scotland)* 3 March 1996, 18 Aug 1996. Cat thieves *D. Telegraph* 19 Sept 1988, *S. People* 5 Jun 1977, *S. Express* 10 Apr 1983, Blackie *Weekend Telegraph* 31 Dec 1994. Holy cat *D. Telegraph* 28 Jan 1995. Praying cat *Economist* 11 Mar 1989, *S. Express* 9 Mar 1986. Couch potato bear *Toronto Globe & Mail* 16 Aug 1995. TV addicts *Sun* 26 Oct 1988, *W'hampton Exp ress & Star* 26 jun 1995, *B'ham Eve. Mail* 6 March 1995. Key dog *D. Telegraph* 27 Jan 1996. Pussy talk *S. People* 2 Aug 1981, *Weekend* 3-9 Mar 1971. Bear verbals *Times* 10 Jul 1985. Political goat *[R]* 17 Sept 1996. Metropigeons *New Scientist* 2+16+30 Sept 1995. Diabetes dog *D. Telegraph* 4 Apr 1996, *Canberra Times* 29 May 1992.

SWEET REVENGE

Wired racoon *Toronto Globe & Mail* 9 May 1981. Dog *Guardian* 26 Jul 1995. Death dog *D. Record* 3 Dec 1993. Attack rabbit *Today* 25 May 1991. Cat-astrophe *Toronto Sun* 2 Aug 1996. Cat pack *San Francisco Chronicle* 31 Dec 1993, Killer collar *[AFP]* 5 Jan 1997. Monoxide mice *Today* 28 Dec 1993. Wild woodchuck *Int. Herald Tribune* 9 Sept 1995. Mouse D. Telegraph. Snake et *The Sun* 24 Mar 1982, *S. Express* 30 Jul 1972. Snake bit *India Today* 31 Jul 1996. Snake strangled *Wolverhampton Express & Star* 21 Aug 1978. Festering ferret *D. Mail* 27 Apr 1991. Deer damage *Grit* 11 Jan 1981, *NY Post* 28 Oct 1993, *European* 23 Aug 1991. Goldfish *D. Star* 26 Dec 1994. Scorpion tea *[AP]* 9 Sep 1996. Boiled hippo *D. Mirror* 17 Jul 1984.

PISSED AGAIN

Gone goat *S. People* 3 Nov 1995. Smoking goat *New Scientist* 5 Mar 1994. Monkey drunk *Weekend* 15-21 Jun 1977. Pissed parrot *The Scotsman* 7 Jan 1986, *Black Country Eve. Mail* 20 Apr 1996. Coke bear *Attleboro' MA Sun-Chronicle* 23 Dec 1985. Boozing bears *St. Catherine's Standard* 24 Dec 1985, *S. Express* 12 Jan 1986. Psycho squirrel *D. Mirror* 21 Jan1983. Ripped rat *D. Mirror* 3 Dec 1994. Pissed pig *Western D. Press* 23 Mar 1996. Pig bender *The Times of Malta* 9 Feb 1996. Ripped horse *Guardian* 14 Oct 1982. Addled asses *Toronto Globe & Mail* 8 Nov 1995. Drunken cock *News of the World* 2 Mar 1997. Plastered cows *The Standard* 17 Oct 1984 *D. Mail* 28 Jan 1983, *Western Morn. News* 15 Dec 1994 *Independent* 18 Feb 1995, *Spotlight on Zimbabwe* 5 Dec 1982, *Niagara Falls Review* 4 Feb 1981. Stoned baboons *Times* 21 Sept 1996, *N/C Journal* 2 Mar 1997. Pissed pachyderm *Celebrity* 4 Aug 1988. Alky elephants *S. Mail* 9 Apr 1995, *Harare Herald* 1 Apr 1995. Jumbo amphetamines *Bangkok Post* 5 May 1993.

GOODBYE CRUEL WORLD

High-rise *Europa Times* Sept 1994. Hang-vultures *Edin. Eve. News* 3 May 1996. Thai toad terror *Omaha World Herald* 24 Dec 1967. Topped turkeys *News of the World* 23 Dec 1979. Sheep snuff *D. Telegraph* 14 Dec 1978, Mongolian massacre *D. Yomiuri (Japan)* 4 Aug 1995 Squirrel squash *D. Telegraph* 14 Sept 1995. Mouse mass deaths *D. Mirror* 20 Dec 1985. Wasted walruses *[AP]* 3 Aug 1996. Wooly jumper *S. Mail*

21 Apr 1996. Diving dogs D. Mirror 19 Oct 1985, D. Post 5 Jan 1995.
Dead-icated dachshund D. Star 17 Oct 1991. Flapping fish S. Express
31 Oct 1982. Stiff Sammy D. Telegraph 17 Aug 1989, D. Mirror 4 Apr
1992. Quake fish Victoria (BC) Times-Colonist 30 Sept 1994. Flaming
fish New Straits Times 9 Jun 1981. Back cat USA Today 29 Jul 1983.
Pig zap LA Times 2 Jun 1994. Back bacon Country Vol 4 (7) Feb/Mar
1991. Frozen chicken Saginaw News 24 Feb 1995. Croakapi [AP] 10
Aug, 7 Sept 1994. Zap cow Yorkshire Post 5Mar 1992, Lewiston (ME)
Sun-Journal 16 Jan 1993, D. Mirror 14 Feb 1973.

TOO MUCH MONKEY BUSINESS
Scrumpers E. Standard 30 Aug 1996, Edinburgh Eve. News 15 Dec
1992. Looters S. Express 14 Sept 1980. Counters S. Mail 3 Mar 1996.
Porno S. Express 9 Oct 1994, Sussex Eve. Argus 30 Jun 1995, S. Mail
21 Jul 1994. Ape rape New Scientist 19 Mar 198, Halifax Eve. Courier
10 Apr 1995. Stripping orang [AFP] 21 Oct 1992. Sexy orang [AFP]
19 Mar 1997. Rogue romeo Independent 28 May 1994. Rail ape
Weekend 13 Jul 1977, S. Mail 7 Jul 1996. Ape broker NY Post 8 Sept
1995. Ape art Guardian 25 May 1995, D. Mirror 3 Nov 1995.
Motorchimp Sydney Sun 14 Jan 1981, Express & Star 6 Dec 1984.
Rogue Victoria BC Times Colonist 27 Oct 1996. Condom monkey
[Reuters] 19 Nov 1993. Cash monkey Katmandu Post 4 Jan 1996.
Monkey mourners [AP] 15 Dec 1995. Killer baboons Victoria [BC]
Times-Colonist 1 Dec 1996. Road rage monkeys Ashbury Park Press 28
Mar 1988, Lincoln [NB] Journal 11 May 1988. Tables turned Herald
Tribune 17 Jun 1980. Monkey politics Observer 31 Mar 1996.

ANIMAL CRACKERS
Gay storks D. Telegraph 29 Jun 1995. Backs D. Star 10 Jun 1981,
Reveille 15 Jun 1977. Talking goat Sun 2 Dec 1996. Fainters D.
Telegraph 10 & 13 Apr 1991. Sheep's bum Guardian 14 Jun 1995.
Hermaphrogoat Rocky Mountain News 9 Mar 1995. Skulldoggery News
of the World 22 May 1994. Hibernating cow Belfast Telegraph 17 Feb
1990. Baldness cure Weekly World News 9 Dec 1986. Liberty parrot
Bild 3 Aug 1989. Pig bang [Reuters] 21 Aug 1993. Elephant poop Times
of Malta 9 Jan 1997, D. Mirror 20 Jan 1997. Art critic D. Telegraph 15
Feb 1997. Aquachick [Reuters] 30 May 1984. Crow plague S. Times 9

Jul 1995, Time 8 Jul 1996. Polar puppy *Wolverhampton Express & Star* 8 Mar 1993. Ear song *The Vetinary Record* 6 & 20 Jan 1996, *D. Telegraph* 28 Apr 1995. Gopher Hole *Newsweek* 24 Jun 1996.